SLAYER OF GODS

SLAYER OF GODS

LYNDA S. ROBINSON

Published by Warner Books

A Time Warner Company

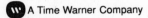

Mysterious Press books are published by Warner Books, Inc., 1271 Avenue of the Americas, New York, NY 10020.

Visit our Web site at www.twbookmark.com

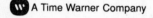 A Time Warner Company

The Mysterious Press name and logo are registered trademarks of Warner Books, Inc.

Printed in the United States of America

First Printing: June 2001

10 9 8 7 6 5 4 3 2 1

Library of Congress Cataloging-in-Publication Data
Robinson, Lynda Suzanne.
    Slayer of gods / by Lynda S. Robinson.
        p.   cm.
    ISBN: 0-89296-705-6
    I. Meren, Lord (Fictitious character)—Fiction. 2. Egypt—History—Eighteenth dynasty, ca. 1570–1320 B.C.—Fiction. 3. Nefertiti, Queen of Egypt, 14th cent. B.C.—Fiction. I. Title.

PS3568.O31227 S55 2001
813'.54—dc21   00-055894

To my uncle, David Womack,
whose love of family and sense of honor
remind me of the qualities
so valued by the ancient Egyptians.

Acknowledgments

I would like to thank Dr. Bill Petty of Museum Tours for reading this manuscript, for his help in imaging the details of everyday life in ancient Egypt, and for an unforgettable tour of Egypt. I'm grateful to him for doing what I thought impossible—getting me to Horizon of the Aten. Bill, you would have made a great advisor or general to King Tutankhamun. I would also like to express my appreciation to two Egyptians, Mostafa and Khaled, for their expertise and hospitality.

I am also indebted to Dr. James Allen, Curator, Department of Egyptian Art, the Metropolitan Museum of Art, New York, for his insights into the events in the waning years of Akhenaten's reign, and most especially his research regarding the fate of Queen Nefertiti. Readers will find his article, "Akhenaten's 'Mystery' Coregent and Successor" fascinating (in *Amarna Letters*, Volume I, KMT Communications, San Francisco, 1991).

I would also like to thank the members of Chicago House, the University of Chicago mission in Luxor, Egypt, for their gracious reception, especially Dr. Carlotta Maher and Dr. Raymond Johnson, director. From them I learned the unhappy news that the great temples at Karnak and Luxor are in even greater danger than most people realize. It may be that—despite the valiant efforts of the Egyptian government and archaeological missions from around the world—

many magnificent reliefs will be gone in a short fifty years. Many factors contribute to the loss of such archaeological treasures—a rising water table and modern pollutants among them. It is a great comfort to those of us who admire the achievements of our ancient ancestors that so many archaeologists, both Egyptian and non-Egyptian, are striving to save this unique cultural heritage.

In Egyptology researchers are constantly uncovering new information, but in the Amarna period—with which this series deals—our knowledge is often sketchy. The story that follows is based on one of several theories of events that took place during the reign of Akhenaten. As always, any errors of fact are mine.

Historical Note

The events upon which *Slayer of Gods* is based took place in mid-fourteenth century B.C. when one of history's unique individuals inherited the throne of Egypt—Akhenaten, the heretic king. It was Akhenaten who took the unprecedented step of abandoning the worship of Egypt's ancient gods, especially the one called Amun. Eventually he even disestablished Amun's powerful priesthood in favor of a minor sun deity called the Aten.

The temple of Amun had benefited from royal patronage since—under the god's banner—Akhenaten's ancestors overthrew foreign rule and established the New Kingdom. Now it was fabulously rich and even owned foreign cities and slaves by the tens of thousands. Such a rich temple had to have been a rival to pharaoh's power.

Strife between Akhenaten and his enemies became so grave that the king had to move the royal court and government away from the centers of traditional power—Thebes and Memphis. He built an entirely new city filled with soaring monuments to pharaoh's new god and beautiful, expressive art. It was called Horizon of the Aten, and there Akhenaten remained, growing more and more fanatical in his persecution of Amun, until he died.

Akhenaten's chief queen was the hauntingly beautiful Nefertiti. She plays a prominent role in the reliefs of her husband's reign and may have wielded a great deal of actual

power. She bore the king six daughters, and it is the affec-
tionate scenes of the royal couple with their children that
are among the most poignant in Egyptian art.

After the twelfth year of Akhenaten's reign, Queen Nefertiti's figure mysteriously vanishes from royal monuments
and correspondence. The reason for her disappearance is unknown. Akhenaten followed his beautiful queen in death a
few years later. After a brief period of uncertainty during
which another brother of Akhenaten called Smenkhare may
have ruled, the boy king Tutankhamun inherited the throne
of Egypt.

Tutankhamun (first known as Tutankh*aten*) was either
Akhenaten's younger brother or his son. He succeeded when
he was between the ages of nine and sixteen and soon began
a complete reversal of Akhenaten's policies. The royal court
moved back to Memphis, and Amun was restored. Tragi-
cally, Tutankhamun died young after a reign of ten years,
leaving his successors to carry out the restoration he began.

Chronology with Selected New Kingdom Rulers of the Late Eighteenth and Early Nineteenth Dynasties

	Years B.C.
Late Predynastic	c. 3000
Early Dynastic	
Dynasties 1–2	?–2649
Old Kingdom	
Dynasties 3–8	2649–2134
First Intermediate Period	
Dynasties 9–10	2134–2040
Middle Kingdom	
Dynasties 11–12	2134–1797
Second Intermediate Period	
Dynasties 13–17	1783–1626
New Kingdom	
Dynasties 18–20	1550–1143

Late Dynasty 18	
Amunhotep III*	1391–1353
Amunhotep IV/Akhenaten	1353–1335
Smenkhare	1335–1333
Tutankhamun	1333–1323
Ay	1323–1319
Early Dynasty 19	
Horemheb	1319–1307
Ramesses I	1307–1306
Seti I	1306–1290
Ramesses II	1290–1224

Third Intermediate Period and Late Period	
Dynasties 21–30	1070–343
Conquest of Egypt by Alexander	332

This chronology does not reflect the possibility espoused by many scholars that there was an extended co-regency during which Akhenaten shared the throne with his father, Amunhotep III. A co-regency is assumed in the context of the Lord Meren series so that it is possible that Tutankhamun was the son of Amunhotep III.

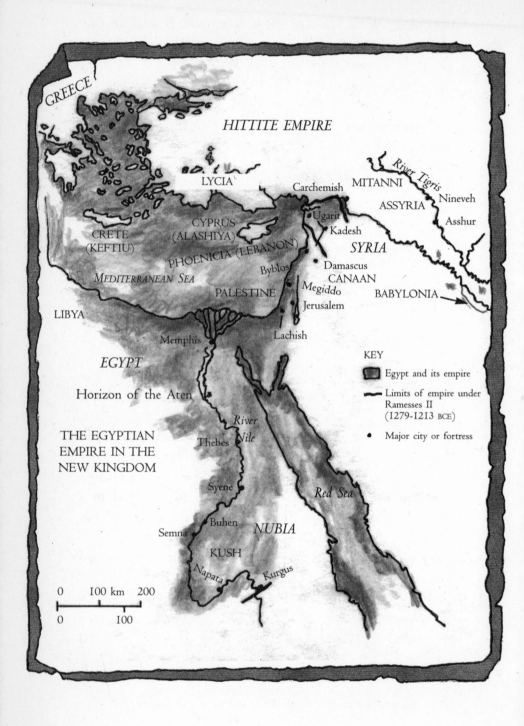

GREECE

HITTITE EMPIRE

LYCIA

River Tigris

MITANNI

Carchemish

Nineveh

ASSYRIA

Ugarit

Asshur

CYPRUS
(ALASHIYA)

Kadesh

CRETE
(KEFTIU)

SYRIA

PHOENICIA (LEBANON)

Mediterranean Sea

Byblos

Damascus

CANAAN

PALESTINE

Megiddo

BABYLONIA

LIBYA

Jerusalem

Memphis

Lachish

KEY

EGYPT

Egypt and its empire

Horizon of the Aten

Limits of empire under
Ramesses II
(1279-1213 BCE)

*River
Nile*

Major city or fortress

THE EGYPTIAN
EMPIRE IN THE
NEW KINGDOM

Thebes

Syene

Red Sea

Buhen

NUBIA

Semna

KUSH

Napata

Kurgus

0   100 km   200

0   100

Chapter I

Memphis, year five of the reign of the pharaoh Tutankhamun

Beauty the goose shuffled slowly through the forest of legs that blocked her way. She fixed her shortsighted gaze on the hard-packed earth in search of the occasional cricket. Around her, in the breezy coolness of late evening, servants gossiped in the kitchen yard. Oblivious to the sounds of lute, harp, and flute that floated from the house, Beauty never paused in her quest even when she encountered feet arrayed in a line in front of her. Above her women's voices droned on, chattering and laughing.

Beauty's small, flat head and beak remained pointed toward the ground. She took another step and pecked at a bare toe. Never lifting her beady gaze from the spot directly in front of her, Beauty took two more waddling steps, eyed another set of toes, and snapped at them. They danced out of her way.

She continued down the line of toes, never lifting her head, never varying from her course, certainly not avoiding the feet, until she reached the back gate. There she nipped at the ankle of the porter in one last ill-tempered and satisfying attack before she sauntered beyond the high wall that enclosed Golden House, the great mansion of Lord Meren, the Eyes and Ears of Pharaoh, Friend of the King, and advisor to the young ruler of the Egyptian empire, Tutankhamun.

Had she been a young, fat goose, Beauty would have soon ended up stewing in a pot. But since she was a pet, everyone had to put up with her menacing ways. She lived up to her name, however. The boldly patterned plumage on her head attracted attention. She had a black crown, hind neck, and facial marks against a white face, a black lower breast, and russet cheek patches and upper breast. Her short, thick neck was no hindrance to her bullying ways, nor was her small bill.

Not long after the goose terrorized the kitchen staff the animal's owner came into the yard, her pace quick in spite of swollen joints and frail bones. "Beauty, where are you? Come to your mother, my little daub of honey."

Satet passed among the servants congregated in the kitchen yard calling the goose's name. She questioned many, always receiving a wave in the direction in which the goose had traveled, and receiving as well complaints from those ambushed by her evil-tempered pet.

"You know she's aged," Satet replied. "You should get out of her way."

Hurrying toward the gate, Satet nodded at the guard.

"You're not supposed to go wandering," he said. "You know Lord Meren dislikes it."

"I'm not going to get lost again," Satet retorted. "I'm

searching for Beauty, and she can't have gone far, so I'll be back quickly."

Before the guard could reply, Satet scurried into the dark street, muttering to herself. "Lord Meren indeed. He cares about me only because my sister served Queen Nefertiti."

The old woman took a deep breath and let it out slowly. The furnacelike heat of day had ebbed from the hard ground beneath her feet, and her mood lightened the farther she walked from the gate. She was weary of being confined to the grounds of Golden House. True, it was a great estate within the city of Memphis, but Satet liked to travel about, visit the markets, docks, temples, and the wells at which people congregated to exchange news.

It was also true that her wits tended to wander a bit, but she wasn't mad and didn't deserve to be pestered and watched all the time. After all, it had been her sister, Hunero, who'd been Queen Nefertiti's favorite cook. Lord Meren said Hunero had poisoned the queen's food, but Hunero had been murdered too, and now Meren wanted Satet to tell him anything she could about Hunero's life that might be of use. But Satet didn't remember anything important. How could she? Queen Nefertiti had died years ago—eleven according to Lord Meren. Or was it longer? Oh, it wasn't important, because the lives and doings of great ones had nothing to do with her. Exploration was far more interesting.

Ever since Lord Meren brought her here from the country Satet had taken advantage of the opportunity to see the sights of pharaoh's greatest city, the capital of the vast Egyptian empire. Looking for Beauty when she wandered away served as the perfect excuse to explore the city.

Satet glanced up and down the street. Moonlight showed nothing to her left, but to her right she glimpsed something on the ground. Satet picked up a scrap of flat bread, the

remnants of someone's meal devoured in a hurry while on
the run. Beauty was following a trail of food. Setting off
down the street, Satet shook her head and grumbled.

"Wouldn't have to sneak off to enjoy myself if that boy
would leave me alone."

She always called Lord Meren "boy," ever since they'd first
met in her sister's old house. He'd been suspicious of Hunero
from the beginning, and once that boy got hold of an idea,
he didn't let loose until he was completely satisfied he knew
everything there was to know. Only last night he'd been after
her again to recall Hunero's doings when she'd worked for
Queen Nefertiti.

It wasn't fair, because Satet hadn't been there. Hunero had
been far away, in the queen's household in the city called
Horizon of the Aten. Satet hardly recalled anything her sister said about what went on in that city in the middle of
nowhere. Oh, she knew it had been built by Nefertiti's husband, the heretic pharaoh Akhenaten, who had nearly destroyed Egypt with his attempts to banish the old gods in
favor of his own. But Satet had barely listened to Hunero's
ramblings about the old days at Horizon of the Aten. It
had nothing to do with her.

"Can't help it if I don't remember," Satet whined to herself. "Hunero was always bragging about being in service to
the queen—may she live forever with the gods—but that
was years ago. Who can remember all her boasts?"

Satet turned into another street. This one was wider, with
old houses on either side that leaned toward each other.
Ahead of her someone stepped into a house and closed the
door, leaving the street deserted. If she shouted for Beauty,
she'd rouse the whole street and get into trouble, so she half
whispered, half hissed.

"Beauty!"

A flap of wings answered her, and Satet caught sight of Beauty as she snapped up something from the street and gobbled it down. The little beast had almost reached the well on the far end of the street. Satet hurried. She was approaching her seventieth year and had to stop a couple of times to catch her breath. The second time, she slowed her pace because Beauty was busy eating something beside the well. No sense hurrying now.

She might get back to the house and have to talk to that boy again. He'd been around too much lately. Wia, one of the family servants, said it was because he'd taken an arrow while fighting a traitor. The wound had festered, causing fever, and demons of infection invaded his body. No doubt the traitor's evil ka, his soul, had tried to avenge itself upon Lord Meren.

Whatever the case, the boy had been confined to his bed, and the whole family had descended upon Golden House. Fear reigned for weeks, but he was strong, his ka equal to the challenge of fighting off the demons of disease. Now he was recovering, which meant that he had the strength to pester Satet. After being subjected to several sessions of his meaningless questions, Satet had finally lost her temper the previous evening.

"Why do you keep asking me these things? I don't know if Hunero spoke to any strangers during the queen's illness. Why don't you ask her?" When Meren reminded her that Hunero was dead, she'd fended him off. "Then why don't you go to Syene and ask the queen's bodyguard? Sebek ought to know more than anyone. Quit pestering me, boy."

Satet was proud of herself for thinking about Sebek. The bodyguard was probably dead, but if a journey to the great southern city of Syene would take Meren away from the house, she wouldn't have to listen to him for a good long time. Of course, his daughter Bener would try to stop him from traveling. She wanted him to rest. She said he wasn't well enough to walk around his garden, much less go on a journey. When her father wouldn't listen to her and insisted on joining his charioteers in the practice yard, Bener had brought in an ally, Lady Bentanta.

A childhood friend of Meren's, Bentanta wasn't intimidated by him as most were. She'd come in response to a message from Bener and had spoken a few words to the invalid in a low whisper. The great Lord Meren, Friend of the King, warrior and royal confidant, had immediately left the practice yard and retired.

"Wonder what she said to him," Satet muttered to herself.

Whatever it had been, it was powerful enough to keep the boy in his bed. Lady Bentanta had remained at his side for almost a week, and during that time they fought. Then one day shouts had erupted from the boy's chamber. Lady Bentanta burst out of the room, turned around and yelled. Satet had never heard anyone yell at Meren. Everyone held him in awe and quite a few feared him. But not Bentanta. She'd stood in his doorway with her hands on her hips and shouted.

"If you don't rest, I'll be back!"

"A fearsome threat," came the bellowed reply. "To avoid another of your visitations, I'd stay in this bed as still as a corpse on the embalmer's table for a year!"

After that scene Meren's mood got worse. That's when pharaoh sent a troupe of musicians to cheer his friend. They'd been so successful that Bener now had them play every night until her father was lulled to sleep. Once he'd regained his full strength he'd be off chasing murderers and other evildoers. The possibility cheered Satet as she reached the well.

It was so late that no one was around the well, except

Beauty. She joined the goose beside the well and saw that her pet was feasting on crumbled fig bread. Someone had been careless.

Beauty was almost finished eating. Satet tried to pick up a piece of the fig bread, but the goose nipped at her fingers and honked.

"Naughty girl!"

As she bent to try again, she heard something behind her. Satet turned her head only to encounter a moving shadow. It swooped at her, and her head burst into dazzling pain. Beauty screeched and flapped her wings when Satet fell beside her. The bird scuttled out of the way before her owner hit the ground. Dazed, aware of little but the agony in her head, Satet felt her body leave the ground. She opened her eyes, glimpsed the yawning blackness beyond the spiral stairs leading to the base of the well, and felt her body drop. She cried out as her head banged against the side of the well. Darkness deeper than that of the well enveloped her as she hit the water.

In the street above, Beauty the goose fussed and flapped and attacked bare toes. She honked and launched herself out of the way when her assailant tried to bash her with a long-handled weapon. The blow landed on packed earth with a crack. Beauty spread her wings, sprang into the air, and flew out of reach. The attacker cursed the goose, looked over the edge of the well at the body floating in the water, and faded into the shadows.

Meren rose from his bed and shoved aside the sheer curtains that hung from the frame surrounding it. The vent in the roof caught the night breeze and funneled it into the room as he listened to the quiet. In a house this size, with its gardens, kitchens, stables, barracks, and servant's quarters, silence was a rarity. He fumbled around until his hand met a table of cedar inlaid with ivory. Using it to steady himself, Meren cursed quietly.

An old nightmare had torn him from sleep as it had many times since his eighteenth year. Usually his own gasps and moans jolted him to consciousness while at the same time pain lanced through his wrist. Now he turned his face to the cool wind issuing from the vent and gulped in air. He tried to calm the racing voice of his heart. Sweat covered his body, and he shivered. In the darkness his fingers searched out the scar on his wrist; it always hurt after he had the dream.

In the night vision he was back in Horizon of the Aten, and his father had just been executed for refusing to abandon the old gods in favor of the pharaoh Akhenaten's new one, the Aten, who was the sun disk. It had been midday, but the city had fallen silent in the way that small creatures do when they sense the presence of a predator. Meren was alone in his house except for a few servants, and his father hadn't been dead more than a few days. Without warning shouts broke the unnatural silence, and Akhenaten's guards burst in and dragged him into the streets.

They took him to a cell near the palace. For days they'd beaten him and asked questions to which he had no answer, certain he was a traitor to pharaoh's new religion. Suspicion had become a sickness with Akhenaten, for Egypt refused to believe in the Aten and clung to the old gods who had created and governed her for thousands of years. As the firstborn son of a traitor, Meren was suspected of aiding the rebellious priests of Amun, the king of the old gods.

After days of starvation and beatings, he hadn't cared when his tormentors came into his cell to kill him. He lay on the floor, naked, his wounds caked with dirt, his vision blurred with sweat, and watched several pairs of feet walk toward him. Rough hands lifted him, and he bit his lip to keep from crying out at the pain. They dragged him into another room where dancing shadows cast by torches made him dizzy.

A cold hand lifted his chin, and Meren opened his eyes to stare into those of Akhenaten. Black as netherworld darkness, brittle as obsidian, those eyes raked him as if trying to divine the very essence of his ka, his soul. Then Akhenaten began to speak, saying that Queen Nefertiti's father had defended Meren.

"Ay speaks on your behalf. He says you're young enough to be taught the truth. My majesty thinks not, but the One God, my father, commands me to be merciful to our children." Akhenaten toyed with a lock of Meren's hair. "We will ask once, Lord Meren. Do you accept the Aten, my Father, as the one true god?"

Meren blinked and swiveled his head. There was Ay, standing silent, looking hard at him. Meren stared into the eyes of his mentor and gave his head a slight shake. Ay was asking him to bring damnation upon his ka. Father had died rather than risk his eternal soul; could he do less? But Ay wanted him to live; Meren could see it in his eyes. And may the gods forgive him, Meren wanted to live.

That was when he'd opened his dry cracked mouth and said, "The Aten is the one true god, as thy majesty has pronounced."

Ay nodded to him, but the movement was so slight that Meren could have imagined it.

"Words come easily for you," the king said as he turned away, "but my Father has shown me a way to claim your ka for the truth. Bring him."

The guards dragged him after the king and stopped before a man who crouched behind a glowing brazier. Meren's vision filled with the red and white glow of the fire. Without warning, he was thrown to the floor on his back. This time he couldn't stop the cry that burst from him as his raw flesh hit the ground. A heavy, sweating body landed on his chest. Meren bucked, trying to throw the man off, but the guard was twice his weight.

He could see the brazier and, beyond it, the fine pleats of pharaoh's robe and the edge of a gold sandal. He fought the guards when they spread out his right arm. In spite of his resistance, the arm was pinned so that his wrist was exposed. The man behind the brazier lifted a white-hot brand. A guard knelt on his upper arm, making it go numb.

Although he couldn't see his arm, Meren felt a wet cloth wipe the flesh of his wrist, saw the brand lift in the air. It was the Aten, the sun disk, whose symbol was a circle with sticklike rays extending from it and ending in stylized hands. The glowing sun disk poised in the air, then the guard pressed the hot metal to Meren's arm.

There was a brief moment between the time the brand met his flesh and the first agony. In that moment, Meren smelled for the first time the odor of burning flesh. Then he screamed. Every muscle convulsed while the guard held the brand to his wrist. When it was taken away Meren broke out in a sweat, and he shivered. Pain from his wrist rolled over him.

He lost consciousness briefly, and when he opened his eyes, the man who'd branded him was smearing a salve on his burned flesh. The pain receded as he was lifted and held so that he faced the king. Akhenaten's black fire eyes burned into him as no brand ever could. Pharaoh took Meren's hand, turned it to expose the mutilated wrist, and examined the crimson symbol of his god. He placed Meren's hand in Ay's.

"He is yours now. But remember, my majesty will know if the boy is false. If he falters from the true path, he dies."

He dies. Meren shook his head and tried to banish the sound of Akhenaten's voice, high, hard, like the sound of a metal saw drawn against granite. Oh, yes, he still remembered that voice even after sixteen years.

Rubbing the back of his neck, Meren shivered and stepped out of the path of the night breeze. There had been something different about this night's evil dream. At the last, when the brand burned into his flesh, something strange happened to him. Suddenly it was as if he'd left his body and floated, invisible, beside the tortured figure on the floor. Only the prisoner who suffered at his feet wasn't himself. It was Tutankhamun. The boy king writhed in agony, screaming, his dark, haunted eyes wide with terror, his body streaked with blood, dirt, and sweat.

"Damnation." Meren paced back and forth beside the bed.

What did this new vision mean? He couldn't consult a magician priest and expose the fact that he'd dreamed about the living god of Egypt.

"Calm yourself, you fool," he muttered. "You dream about things that worry you. You always have."

And he'd been worried about pharaoh for some time. Only fourteen, Tutankhamun had lost most of his family, including his mother, Queen Tiye, and the woman he thought of as a second mother, his brother's wife, Nefertiti. Now that he knew the queen had been murdered, Tutankhamun grieved anew for Nefertiti's loss. He'd been very young during his brother's reign and so had understood nothing of the violent hatreds engendered by the Aten heresy. Tutankhamun remembered Akhenaten as a doting older sibling, a limitless source of toys, sweets, and exciting chariot rides.

Akhenaten's sudden death had brought both confusion and relief to Egypt, but after a period of turbulence during which the next heir, Smenkhare, succumbed to illness, Tutankhamun became king. Inheriting the throne of Egypt and becoming a living god who controlled a vast and fabulously rich empire had been a formidable task for the boy. But he'd succeeded, only to find himself condemned to opulent isolation. Grave, beautiful, and headstrong, Tutankhamun had faced the burdens heaped upon him with courage, but in the last few months those burdens had grown. Evildoers had desecrated the bodies of Akhenaten and Nefertiti in their tomb at Horizon of the Aten.

Tutankhamun had faced that crisis and endured, but after years of trying hard to be a great king, he was beginning to show signs of strain. More and more he would slip out of the palace with a single guard to accompany him and seek relief in escapades that terrified his ministers. So far no harm had come to the king, but how long could this good fortune continue?

What was worse, Meren could see the strain in the king's face. During an audience or ceremony at a temple he would see a distant look come over Tutankhamun, and Meren knew he was thinking of Nefertiti, wondering who could have killed his beloved second mother. He was wondering if her ka wandered lost and mad in the desert, as the souls of unavenged victims were said to do. Did she haunt the boy's dreams, visit him and cry out for vengeance? Meren saw evidence of it when he looked at the king, in the shadows beneath those large, somber eyes. And then Meren would wonder—how long could the living god, who was after all a mortal boy as well, continue to bear this intolerable burden before he succumbed?

Meren shook his head, went to a chest and pulled out a

kilt, which he belted around his hips. He covered the Aten brand on his wrist with a leather band. Finding Nefertiti's killer was urgent. As strong and brave as the king was, he was far too young to endure such anguish and the torture of uncertainty for long. The only solution was to find the truth and present it to the king. If Meren could give Tutankhamun the murderer, perhaps the boy could find peace. Perhaps Meren could find some peace as well.

Still rubbing the brand on his wrist beneath the leather band, Meren left his bedchamber. He wasn't going to get any more sleep, so he slipped out of the house with a brief command to his own guards to be silent regarding his absence. During his enforced rest he'd gone on long walks in the hours before dawn before his daughter Bener was awake. Arguing with her tired him as no exercise could.

This would be his last walk, a test of strength before he went in search of Nefertiti's favorite bodyguard, Sebek. He'd had his men searching for the queen's old servants, including Sebek, for some time, but they'd been unable to locate him. However, his persistence and patience with Satet had borne fruit unexpectedly when the old woman had mentioned the guard last night. He'd been surprised that she remembered Sebek, but her memory tended to appear and disappear like the ephemeral clouds in the Egyptian sky. Learning Sebek's whereabouts was a good sign. Perhaps the guard knew something that at last would reveal the identity of Nefertiti's murderer.

He left the house and walked down the avenue between the two reflection pools to the gate. He glanced at the water lilies floating on the surface of the water, their buds closed and invisible. He heard a fish snap at an insect and felt a tiny spray of water drops. He reached the gate. One of his guards let him out, and he set off in the direction of the temple of Ptah, the god of the city, thinking as he walked.

He knew who had supplied the poison to Nefertiti's cook, Hunero, but someone else had conceived of the idea of killing the queen. Nefertiti had been engaged in a dangerous attempt to reconcile her husband with the old gods of Egypt. Losing her had nearly sent Egypt into chaos along with her pharaoh. That had been more than eleven years ago.

Now Tutankhamun was king, and bore the responsibility for healing Egypt's open wounds. Some who had suffered at Akhenaten's hands wanted to keep those wounds open and bleeding. It was this group who fostered the unspoken belief that the boy was tainted with the blood of a line that had nearly destroyed Egypt. Tutankhamun lived with the certainty that they wanted to rid the throne of its tainted occupant. A heavy burden for a boy not yet fifteen.

Meren shook his head as he remembered how, despite these adversities, the king was determined to become the epitome of a warrior king. In pursuit of this ideal he'd insisted on going with the army on a raid against an outlaw band. The boy had taken too many risks in that skirmish. Tutankhamun was the incarnation of the king of the gods, but he was still mortal. A bandit's arrow could kill him in an instant, and then what would happen to Egypt?

Turning down the avenue that led to the temple, Meren breathed deeply, taking in air laden with moisture. The floodwaters of the Nile were receding, and soon pharaoh's surveyors would spread across the land to remeasure field boundaries and estimate crop yields. During inundation the population of Memphis swelled with laborers from the country ordered into the service of temple and government projects. Royal granaries and supply houses dispensed vast quantities of grain, wheat, barley, oil, and other commodities to pay such workers who would otherwise have little to do.

Indeed, it was a busy time of the year for pharaoh's ministers, including Meren's old mentor, Ay. Meren had been concerned for his friend ever since he'd discovered that Nefertiti had been murdered. He had never told Ay of this discovery, and the old man still believed what everyone had assumed when Nefertiti died—that the queen had fallen ill from a plague that had killed her daughters. Meren was reluctant to tell Ay about the murder until he knew who the killer was. If he could capture the one responsible, the old man might bear the news better.

Thinking hard, Meren turned down a side street, away from the temple's massive pylon gate with its carved and painted reliefs and giant doors covered with gold. He would make his way around the walls that surrounded the temple complex and return home. Before an enemy had tried to kill him a couple of months ago he'd been on the track of three suspects, men powerful enough to have arranged the queen's death. Yamen the army officer was dead. Another was the Syrian Dilalu, who sold weapons to anyone rich enough to pay for them. The last was Zulaya, an elusive merchant from one of the Asiatic kingdoms, perhaps Babylon. This was one of the reasons he'd asked that one of the Eyes and Ears of Pharaoh stationed abroad be summoned home. He needed to speak with someone whose task it was to keep an eye on people like Dilalu and Zulaya.

Yamen had been killed before Meren could question him about the queen's murder. An unseen, unknown enemy always preceded him before Meren could question someone who might shed light on the mystery. That someone had caused the deaths of the cook Hunero and her husband. He'd brought Hunero's sister to Memphis in the hope that she might remember something of use, but her memory faltered often. Meren was of the opinion that Satet deliberately forgot things that were inconvenient or frightening to her.

Turning a corner Meren paused, realizing he had taken a wrong turn and was in an unfamiliar area. The neighborhood around the temple was old, as old as the ancient ones who built the pyramids. Over the years the houses and storage buildings had multiplied and expanded, taking up parts of streets and creating a network of roads that dead-ended, alleys that zigzagged and looped back on themselves and burrowed into the warrens of mud brick that served as combination dwellings, mangers, and workshops.

Having taken one wrong turn, Meren now found himself in a narrow little alley that ended in a blank wall. At one time an exterior stair had stood against this wall. Only five mud brick steps remained, leading nowhere. Meren backtracked only to find himself in an alley hardly wide enough for one person to pass, and this took an abrupt turn that went back the way he'd come. Meren stopped and sighed. He would have to find another stair so that he could climb high enough to see where he was from a rooftop. Luckily he spotted one a few houses down. He reached it quickly and set his foot on the bottom step.

"Out for a stroll, is we?"

Whipping around, Meren found the way blocked by a man with the mass of a temple column. Although light was only beginning to permeate the darkness of early morning, he could make out a skewed smile filled with broken teeth and eyes the whites of which had yellowed. Meren's hand went to his side. Where the scabbard for his dagger should have been there was emptiness. He hadn't brought a weapon.

What madness. He always carried a dagger. That cursed nightmare must have disturbed him more than he'd thought.

Meren planted his feet solidly and said, "Go away."

"Not before I get my hands on that pretty belt. Give it to me."

Sighing, Meren waved the man away. "I've no patience with thieves. Leave before I decide you're worth the trouble of dragging you to the city police."

He should have realized the thief was too dim-witted to recognize authority when he encountered it. His rank protected him most of the time. Few commoners would dare speak to him, much less steal something from him. But he'd wandered into the Caverns, the disreputable area of the city near the docks, the denizens of which recognized no higher authority than the edge of a blade. If he hadn't been thinking so hard he would have realized the danger. As it was, his new friend responded to the dismissal by drawing a knife.

"You got one last chance to do what I say. Gimme the belt."

As he finished speaking the man waved the knife at Meren, who grabbed his arm and jammed it against his knee. The thief grunted but didn't let go of the blade. He rammed his fist into Meren's jaw and kneed him. The blow caught Meren in the side at the site of his healing arrow wound. He cried out as his knees buckled. He caught himself by planting his palms on the ground, but fell when his attacker rained blows on him from above. He felt a knee on his back, twisted, and grabbed the thief's arm as the knife came at him. Staring at the tip of the blade, Meren felt his arms quiver from the effort to hold off the man's full force.

Just when he thought his strength would give way, a dagger blade descended from nowhere and settled against the thief's throat. The man went still, his eyes protruding while he made a high-pitched squealing sound.

"Be good enough to stop that, if you please," said a low, easy voice.

Meren felt the thief remove his weight. He sat up as a dark figure herded the thief away from him. The man backed away from the dagger, eyeing the newcomer. Suddenly he growled and took a threatening step toward his enemy. The dagger snaked out and carved a neat X on the thief's belly. He yelped and clutched his stomach.

"Run along now, or I'll have to kill you, and that would be so tiresome."

The thief staggered away from his tormentor, turned, and ran. Meren was too surprised to move. He sat down, his hands braced on the ground, and gaped as his rescuer cleaned the dagger, stuck it in a scabbard, and whirled around to offer a hand.

"Rescuing the great Lord Meren. A most edifying experience after my long absence from Egypt."

Speechless, Meren stared at the small hand with its immaculate nails and the row of gold bracelets above it. He followed the delicate line of an arm to a curved shoulder, and finally his gaze found a smiling mouth of dusky crimson and eyes that tilted up slightly at the outside corners. His amazement grew as he took in a small-boned frame taut with disciplined musculature. His rescuer wore a gown of the finest and softest wool. Red with a blue border, it fastened over one shoulder and cinched at the waist with a belt of lapis lazuli and gold beads. There were few in Egypt who dressed in such a foreign style.

Meren felt a flush burn up his neck to his face. "By all the gods of Egypt. Anath."

"Greetings, Meren."

Before he could get up, Anath grabbed his hand and hauled him to his feet.

To cover his embarrassment at being rescued by a woman, even this woman, Meren busied himself brushing dirt from his kilt. Then he faced her, his features composed. "Welcome back to Egypt, Eyes of Babylon."

Anath cocked her head to the side, planted her fists on her hips, and studied him. Then she laughed.

"You should have seen yourself squirming in the dirt. You've grown soft lolling about here in Egypt."

Feeling his face heat again, Meren decided not to respond to Anath's teasing. She hadn't changed in the two years she'd been away. She found humor in the oddest places. She was the daughter of a concubine, fathered by a nobleman called Nebwawi. Neglected by her elderly father, Anath had roamed the city without escort and turned up at odd places like the royal docks and in temple schools to which only boys were admitted. Nebwawi had been a friend of Meren's father, and Meren had watched Anath grow up. She loved horses, spending more time in the stables than the house, and she could commune with almost any creature—cats, dogs, birds, monkeys, even the royal lions and leopards.

A leopard, that's what she reminded him of, a diminutive hunting cat. Anath had inherited her mother's wildly curling black hair, but her light, gold-brown eyes were unique. Nebwawi came from a family prominent in the delta, where Greeks and Mittannis intermarried with Egyptians. Whatever its origin, Anath's uniqueness served her better than her beauty did. Small yet athletic, she could outshoot many of his charioteers at the bow, and certainly had as much skill in driving a chariot. Still, Meren had never understood what had prompted Ay to train her to be one of the Eyes of Pharaoh. That had been at Horizon of the Aten.

Anath had spent several years under Ay's tutelage. She managed to avoid the notice of the unpredictable Akhenaten, but when pharaoh's behavior became even more erratic, Ay had sent his protégée to Memphis to complete her education. Later she had gone to Tyre, then Byblos, and finally Babylon.

Not yet thirty, Anath was now one of the most successful of the Eyes of Pharaoh under Meren's direction. She lived in Babylon most of the time, posing as the wealthy widow of an Egyptian trader. She had inherited her father's fleet of ships, and they plied their trade at ports like Mycenae in Greece, the cities in Cyprus, and those in the Egyptian empire in Canaan and Palestine. Her wealth gave her power, which in turn gave her access to foreign courts and kings. However, Meren still remembered her as an awkward girl in Horizon of the Aten. Always by herself, neglected and allowed to wander, she'd rush into rooms, late for meals or receptions, sweaty and smelling like horses.

That was all long ago, and now she was looking at him the way she did a lame horse, the way his physician did during an examination. Meren straightened his spine and muttered his thanks for her timely intervention. His charioteers would chuckle behind his back for weeks when they found out he'd needed rescuing by a woman. Irritated, Meren forestalled the questions he could see Anath was going to ask.

"What are you doing in the Caverns at this time of night?"

Anath glanced up at the brightening sky. "I docked yesterday, and I was on my way to see how my horses fared after the long journey home. You know I rise early."

"I remember you hardly slept."

"I sleep," she said with a toss of her head. "I just don't sleep long. Life is too interesting to waste it sleeping, Meren."

Somewhere nearby a donkey brayed, and they heard the

scuffling and muted tap of dozens of sheep's hooves. The new day was beginning. Anath put one hand on the hilt of the dagger at her waist and swept the other in a gesture indicating that Meren should precede her.

"I think I should escort you home. You shouldn't be wandering the streets in your condition."

"How did you know—never mind," Meren said. He shook his head as he led the way out of the alley. "I forgot with whom I was speaking."

"Pharaoh told me you ferreted out a traitor and took an arrow," Anath said as she followed him. "It seems I've come home just in time."

As he walked he looked back at her, scowling. "I asked pharaoh to summon someone to help uncover a murderer, Anath. You're not here to rescue me, by the gods."

As he finished he stepped into an intersection and nearly ran into the path of a woman with a tall water jar balanced on her head. Anath grabbed his arm and pulled him back just in time. Meren tightened his mouth and watched the woman walk by with that steady, smooth gait required to balance a heavy jar. Then he heard Anath chuckle. Setting his jaw, he launched into the street with a quick stride. With luck, he would leave her behind. Three streets later she was still at his heels, and he was the one out of breath. He gave up and slowed down. Anath drew alongside him, unperturbed.

"You must be greatly troubled," she remarked mildly.

"Why do you say that?"

"Why else would you ask me to come home? We both know the king of Babylon is hatching plots with the Hittites, and I'm not going to find out what they are from Memphis."

"You have an able assistant, as I remember. He'll manage until you return. I need to . . ."

His words faded as they came upon the public well near his house. Several men were hefting the sodden body of an old woman up the stairs. Meren hurried to the crowd that surrounded the body as it was laid on the ground. He broke through to see the pale, flaccid features of Satet.

"Stand back," he said to those around him. "Who found this woman?"

"I did, lord," said a woman carrying a water jar. She made a sign against evil and cast a fearful glance at the well. "Poor Satet."

"You knew her?" Meren asked.

"She would come to the well and visit with those who drew water," said the woman. "I came a few moments ago and found her when I got to the bottom of the stairs. She was under the water, just floating there." The woman swallowed hard. "I knew it was too late. She was facedown, and didn't move."

"I see," Meren said as he knelt beside the body.

Behind him he heard Anath talking to the men who had brought the body out of the well. He lifted a length of her soggy white hair. A wound on Satet's forehead might have come had she stumbled on the stairs and hit her head. He'd warned the old one about wandering around the city alone, but she'd managed to slip out by herself again. Shaking his head, Meren stood and gave orders for the body to be taken to his house. His physician, Nebamun, would examine it, but there was little doubt that Satet had drowned. The blow to her head wouldn't have killed her, unless she was more fragile than Meren had thought.

Still, with Nefertiti's killer still free, he could never be certain that a witness like Satet hadn't died by design. Someone could have hit her and dumped her into the well. So many witnesses had ended up dead that he couldn't afford to assume that Satet's demise was an accident. In fact, the more he thought about it, the more certain he became. He didn't believe in convenient accidents or coincidences. Satet's body had abrasions on it where the face and shoulders had scraped against the well, probably as it floated in the water. Or were these signs of a struggle? Nebamun might know.

Whatever the case, his enforced rest was now at an end, no matter how much his family might object. Meren walked around the well, but saw nothing out of the ordinary.

"No one heard her cry out," Anath said, as she rejoined him. "No one heard her fall. Her body was stiff?"

"Yes. I think she died a few hours ago."

"She was a servant of yours?"

Meren leaned against the wall that surrounded the well and surveyed the trampled ground. "You might call her so." He narrowed his eyes as something gleamed in the growing sunlight. "What's that?"

Anath followed the direction of his gaze, picked up an irregularly shaped piece of light-colored pottery and turned it over.

"I don't know," she said.

Meren took it from her. It wasn't pottery after all. He wasn't sure, but he thought it was a piece of ivory.

"What is this doing here?" he murmured to himself.

Anath gave the shell a glance and shrugged. "It's litter, Meren. Like that piece of basket over there, and those shards of pottery."

"Perhaps." Meren slipped the ivory in his belt and shoved away from the wall. As he did so the woman he'd questioned hurried to him and bowed.

"Lord Meren, what will we do? We can't take water from the well."

"Have a magician priest purify it," Anath answered.

Meren nodded. "I'll send someone when I return home."

"The lord is most kind and generous," the woman said.

As he and Anath left, the woman was surrounded by her friends and plied with questions.

Anath glanced at them over her shoulder, then shook her head at Meren. "It seems to be dangerous to live in your household."

"Satet might have tripped on the well stairs, Anath."

"You don't believe that." Her demeanor was calm. Unlike more sheltered women, violent death didn't disturb her.

"She might have tripped," Meren repeated. "But you're right. Since I began to investigate a certain crime, too many people have been killed." Meren glanced at Anath's calm expression. "Have you ever read one of the copies of the inscriptions from the pyramids of the ancient ones? There is one that speaks of great evil—the sky darkens, the vaults of the heavens quiver, and the bones of the earth tremble. If I can't find the one whom I seek, he will cause all that to happen. I fear for the harmony and balance of Egypt."

"One man will do this?"

He stopped and looked down at the Eyes of Babylon. "One man, Anath, succeeded in banishing the gods of Egypt. I no longer ask what one man can do if he has the courage, or the madness with which to accomplish evil."

Chapter 2

By midday Meren had arranged for Satet's embalming and burial in the commoner's necropolis. A consultation with Nebamun, who had examined the body, confirmed Meren's suspicion that there was no way of knowing whether the old woman died by accident or design. The mysterious circumstances behind Satet's death made him even more anxious to get to Syene and find Nefertiti's chief bodyguard.

When he returned from the investigation and burial arrangements, Anath visited with Bener. The Eyes of Babylon swept into his house as if it were her own, calling out to his daughter.

"Bener, where are you? I sail the Great Green to see you, and you're lying about somewhere, I vow!"

Bener had appeared in the main reception hall, eyes wide, mouth open at the sight of Anath. Then she'd given a whoop and launched herself into the older woman's arms. The two had laughed, hugged, and left Meren standing by himself in the lofty chamber while they hurried off to find Kysen.

Slightly annoyed that Anath could dismiss their impending business so easily, Meren muttered to himself. "You'd think she was sixteen instead of twenty-nine, by the gods."

Now Meren was walking beside the reflection pool in the private garden behind the house. Beyond the wall he could hear the rhythmic creak and slosh of the shaduf, the long wooden pole with a bucket at its end that lifted water from a nearby canal. It supplied the pipes and small ditches that fed the garden's pool, trees, and flower beds. The north breeze kept the heat away for the moment, but soon even shade would fail to ward off the power of Ra, the sun. The cool months were still many weeks away, and Meren wished he could speed their arrival. Ordinarily the heat was something he ignored, but during his enforced idleness he'd had time to think about it, which only made his recovery more tedious.

He paused to stare at the rows of incense trees resting in their protective ceramic containers—frankincense, tamarisk, and myrrh shrubs. Anath had been recalled at his request because she was one of the few he could trust with the secret of Nefertiti's murder. She wasn't a member of a rival faction at court, and they were childhood friends. In her offhand and rebellious way she'd always been his ally, ever since that day many years ago when she'd fallen into a canal during a game of chase with her playmates. Meren had plucked her from the water just as a crocodile tried to snatch her in its long, slimy jaws.

He was wasting time in memories. Turning quickly, Meren beckoned to a maid and told her to summon Abu, the commander of his charioteers. When Abu arrived, Meren was leaning against an old horseradish tree.

The charioteer saluted. "Yes, lord."

"Are the preparations made for tomorrow's sailing?"

"There you are." Anath came down the graded path toward him, her gown a bright red contrast to the dappled shadows cast by the shade trees. "Oh, Abu. Greetings."

She sailed past the charioteer with a nod and joined Meren. "What's this about going south? You're not completely healed."

"I'm well enough," Meren said, trying to hold his temper. He was sick of everyone treating him like an old man. "The journey is necessary, and I must speak with you before I leave." He glanced at Abu. "Is everything ready?"

"Yes, lord, but the Lady Bener isn't pleased. She says—"

"Abu, please refrain from telling me what she says."

Unperturbed, Abu nodded and left.

"Aren't you curious about why you were summoned home?" he asked as Anath bent to touch the petals of a cornflower. Once again, he admired her exotic beauty and confident manner.

"The king said you would tell me, and he instructed me not to ask Ay, so I know it's a grave and secret matter." She held his gaze. "The Divine One seems much troubled, distracted even, though he tries to hide it."

"I know that all too well."

Anath suddenly dropped to the ground, crossed her legs, and straightened her skirts. She patted the earth beside her and grinned at him.

"Sit down, Lord Meren, Friend of the King, Eyes and Ears of Pharaoh, and confide in me."

Giving up the effort to impress his guest with the gravity of her position and what he was about to impart, Meren sat.

"My tale begins in Horizon of the Aten. You will remember the last years of Akhenaten when his hatred of the old gods increased with each circuit of the solar boat of Ra."

Anath's merry expression vanished, and her tilted eyes darted around the garden looking for eavesdroppers. "Your father was killed, and so were your cousin's wife and child."

Meren's heart pounded against his ribs, and his mouth tightened. "I speak of the days after. When I served under Ay."

Her brow furrowing, Anath said softly, "I remember. You were often at the palace of the great royal wife, or on some mission of diplomacy for Ay. I was studying the language of the Asiatics."

"You were quite diligent, as I remember," Meren said with a brief smile. "You turned up in the most unexpected places—the royal granaries, the office of correspondence, the barracks."

"I went where there were people who spoke Babylonian." Anath drew her dagger and began tossing it, catching the hilt and tossing it again. "You're greatly troubled, or you wouldn't avoid telling this tale by discussing my activities. Go on, Meren."

The flying dagger was distracting. When Anath threw it into the air again, he snatched it and kept it. "Very well. I'll tell you what I know, and what I have guessed." His memories were so clear, they could have been recorded on papyrus . . .

He remembered the day he and Ay returned from a journey to Thebes only to hear appalling news. Horizon of the Aten was abuzz. From the house of the master sculptor Thutmose, to the great Riverside Palace of pharaoh, people spoke of nothing else. When Ay heard the rumor, he dropped his wine goblet. Meren had been sitting with his mentor in the antechamber before the throne room of the Great Palace, and jumped to his

feet startled. Courtiers and ministers stared at them. Oblivi-
ous, Ay rushed out of the ceremonial center with Meren close
behind. Jumping into his chariot, Ay ordered the driver to the
Riverside Palace, the private residence of the king and queen.
Meren drove after them down the long Royal Road that stretched
across the city. Dust flew in his face, and Meren glanced to
his right. Behind the perpetual haze of suspended dust he glimpsed
the horizon formed by the cliffs to the east. He dared not take
more than a glance, though, because Ay was charging toward
the battlements of the palace as if a desert fiend were after him.

He caught up with Ay at the soaring golden gates in the
perimeter wall. Hurrying to catch up with his mentor, he had
no time to catch his breath as they raced by royal guards, the
queen's steward, Wah, and a shocked chamberlain who tried to
announce them. He finally drew even with Ay as the older
man threw open the doors to his daughter's reception hall. They
halted on the threshold, stunned.

Surrounded by servants and priests, standing in a shaft of
light shining through one of the high windows, Nefertiti turned
to face them. Ordinarily her appearance was startling because
of her beauty—those enormous eyes, fragile jaw, and hollow
cheeks, that long and graceful neck mirrored in even more ele-
gant legs. But what brought them to a standstill was the crown
she wore—the double crown of Upper and Lower Egypt, the
crown of a king.

Meren glanced at Ay. The older man's hands were clenched
at his sides as he stared at the sight. Upon Nefertiti's brow
rested the red crown of Lower Egypt, wide and flaring out to
hold the inner white crown of Upper Egypt. Ay made some
kind of sound only Meren heard, then walked up to his daugh-
ter. With a jerky motion of his hand he dismissed the atten-
dants and priests standing around the queen. Nefertiti hadn't
spoken. She swallowed hard, lifted the crowns from her head,

and set them in a box held by her chief priest, Thanuro. He hesitated, as if he was considering staying, but Meren jerked his head toward the door, and the priest left. In moments they were alone with the great royal wife of Akhenaten.

Ay stared into her eyes and hissed. "Set and Anubis protect us. Are you mad?"

"Do you think this is my idea?" Nefertiti retorted, her voice rising. She pressed her lips together as if to suppress the violence of her emotions. "This was only a fitting. The crowns aren't finished."

"You're going to let him make you pharaoh?" Ay's voice cracked. He took a deep breath and began again. "This is madness."

Throwing up her hands, Nefertiti walked away from them as she spoke. "He says the idea came to him in a vision from the Aten. I am to become king jointly with him. That way he can entrust the daily business of government to me and concentrate on his reformation. You know how he hates diplomacy and administration. It's almost impossible to get him to make decisions about who is to fill various posts or about distribution of grain supplies, much less deal with foreign kings."

Ay stalked over to Nefertiti and grabbed her arm. "You can make those decisions without becoming pharaoh. Women don't become kings. Kings are men, the sons of the great Amun, king of the gods."

"If I'm pharaoh I can make decisions without bothering Akhenaten, which means he won't have to tolerate as many interruptions in his campaign to establish the Aten as the only true god."

Nefertiti gently disengaged Ay's hand from her arm, and Meren saw the glitter of unshed tears in her eyes. "Don't you see? He didn't ask if I wanted to be pharaoh. I have no choice."

Across the gulf of years the words echoed in Meren's mind as he sat beside Anath. *I have no choice.* Had Nefertiti ever had a choice in what befell her?

He glanced at Anath, who had taken back her dagger to polish it with a length of her red robe. "A little more than a year later, she was dead."

"A great pity," Anath said, the dagger resting in her motionless hands. "And a tale of great evil. Akhenaten perverted the rightness of things, Meren, but that's hardly a secret, even if no one speaks of it openly."

"I told you about it because you were too young to know how things were back then. I felt—most of us felt that chaos ruled. Akhenaten was driving Egypt away from harmony and balance, abandoning all that was right and true. In those final years, Nefertiti was trying to bring him to see reason. It was slow, and she had to go carefully, but she thought she could bring about reconciliation with the old gods. She was working with the priests of Amun."

Anath scooted around to face him and whispered. "Do you mean she was actually speaking to them? If the king found out . . ."

"He didn't," Meren said. "But all her work came to nothing because she died."

Nodding, Anath said, "The plague."

"No."

Her eyes became slits as she regarded him silently.

"She was poisoned by her steward, Wah. He supplied the poison, and her favorite cook used it over a period of time until she collapsed."

Anath said a spell against evil under her breath. "By all the demons of the underworld, Meren, what are you saying?" The color ebbed from her face while her breathing sped up. She darted more glances around the garden, then lowered her voice to a whisper. "How do you know this?"

Meren told her about accidentally discovering the truth from Wah before he was killed. "Since then I've been trying to find out who ordered Wah to kill Nefertiti, but every time I come upon someone who might be able to help, they're murdered."

"This is impossible," Anath muttered.

"I assure you, it's not. I wish it were."

Anath stared into his eyes for a long time, as if she could read the truth in their agate darkness. Finally she nodded once, and Meren knew she had accepted what he'd said. She would never question him again.

"I'm going to Syene tomorrow to find the bodyguard Sebek, but I've put it about that I'm sailing for my country house to complete my recovery."

"Send someone else," Anath said with a frown. "You're not strong enough for such a long journey."

"Yes I am, and besides, the matter is urgent. You were right when you said pharaoh is troubled, Anath. He loved Queen Nefertiti as a mother. His ka suffers great torture knowing that she was murdered and that her killer has gone unpunished for so many years. The idea that her majesty's spirit cries out for vengeance torments him. Anyway, I must go because there's no one else. Kysen must remain here to conduct business with the king and to keep an eye on those who may be involved."

"Who?"

"There are several, but two are Asiatics, so I thought you'd know more about them than anyone here. A dealer in weapons called Dilalu, and a merchant named Zulaya."

Getting to her feet, Anath dusted off her gown and leaned against the tree trunk. Folding her arms, she cocked

her head to the side in her characteristic gesture and regarded him solemnly.

"Dilalu is loyal only to himself and to gold. Riches are
his only lust, except for his cat. He'll cast his own father
into the Lake of Fire if paid enough, but he's a coward.
That's why he surrounds himself with mercenaries. I can't
see him ever having the courage to carry out such a blas-
phemy."

"And Zulaya?"

"Zulaya has no interest in the affairs of kings except
when they touch his own dealings. I have had business with
him often in Babylon. If threatened he's capable of killing,
efficiently and without remorse."

"Has he ever mentioned Akhenaten or Horizon of the
Aten?"

Anath shook her head. "He comes to Egypt for trade,
Meren. He has a house here, but he spends more time
abroad than in the Two Lands."

"Someone ordered the queen's murder," Meren snapped
in frustration.

"Isn't it more likely to have been an Egyptian?" Anath
asked with eyebrows raised.

"That's what I assumed until I received information that
pointed to three men—Zulaya, Dilalu, and Yamen, who is
dead."

"Yamen? An officer in the army. A corrupt officer, if
I'm not mistaken. I've heard complaints about him from
some of the Canaanite vassals."

"He was murdered before I could fully question him. He
was still alive when I reached him, but what he said made
no sense."

Anath's gaze fastened on him, and she raised her eyebrows in inquiry.

Meren sighed. "He babbled something about the one who killed him. Yamen said his killer would destroy me as he had him, that all perish who threaten him. He said no one else knew the killer like he did. A familiar refrain. I've heard such claims before from the companions of men of great evil. I hope he wasn't right, or I'll never find the bastard."

Anath shoved away from the tree trunk. Head down, hands clasped behind her back, she walked in a circle without speaking. Then she stopped and looked directly at him.

"Let me think for a while. I might remember something about these men that will help. You've looked at the royal records and questioned the queen's former servants, I take it."

"Those that are still alive. Some are dead. There is no record of what became of many others. With the passage of time many moved around and the royal records don't show where they went. That's what happened with the queen's guard, Sebek."

"Of course."

Anath resumed her slow walk. Meren got up and brushed himself off.

"I have it!" Anath exclaimed.

"What?"

"On your way to Syene stop at Horizon of the Aten and look at the records there."

"Horizon of the Aten is almost completely abandoned. Many of the brick buildings are falling apart."

"But outdated records were left behind in places like the overseers' offices, the royal granaries, and the office of the king's correspondence. I know where a lot of things were kept. I was there often enough. I'll come with you and help you look in the right places."

"I can find them myself," Meren said. "After I see Sebek."

"If I go with you, we can stop on the way to Syene because it won't take as long to search."

"I don't want to take the time."

Anath rolled her eyes. "You can't be certain whether it's more important to see Sebek or find records at Horizon of the Aten. If you're worried about him, send someone to Syene to guard him until you can talk to him."

"I don't see why—"

"Ha!" Anath clapped her hands together. "Now I remember. I knew there was something important about going to Horizon of the Aten. Do you remember old Hapimen, chief scribe of the office of royal records? I used to visit him at his work because he had an assistant, a former slave who could read and write. I would practice my foreign languages by conversing with him while he worked." She drew nearer Meren, her eyes gleaming. "Do you know what he worked on? The queen's correspondence. And I remember where he kept his records, and where he dumped the notes he took when he no longer needed them."

Hesitating, Meren weighed Anath's words.

"We can stop at Horizon of the Aten, pick up the records, and be on our way in a few hours. If we find any important documents we can return on our way back to Memphis."

Meren paced, weighing the risk of delay. "Very well, but if you're coming with me, you'd better wear Egyptian clothing. I'm trying to keep this inquiry a secret, and it won't help if you parade around looking like the goddess Ishtar and call attention to our movements."

Anath planted her fists on her hips again and surveyed him. "Meren, you're dressed in the finest linen Egypt can produce, wearing a gold and carnelian headband and an electrum signet ring. If you aim to move about without attracting notice, you're going to fail."

"I mean I don't wish to provoke curiosity and suspicion."

"Then you should never have become the Eyes and Ears of Pharaoh."

Meren smiled slightly. "My dear Anath, I didn't have a choice."

Chapter 3

Meren lay on his bed with his eyes closed. He wasn't asleep, but he needed to rest. Anath had left soon after their conversation and he'd spent the rest of the day consulting with Kysen. His son would continue to prowl the foreign district in disguise hoping to pick up more information on their suspects. Kysen also would conduct the affairs of the Eyes and Ears of Pharaoh during Meren's absence. The king had given his consent to this arrangement last year when it became clear that Meren's son would make an excellent successor to his confidential inquiry agent.

Bener had tried to convince Meren to delay his journey, and now she was supervising the preparation of the evening meal, grumbling all the while. Meren shifted on the bed, trying to find a more comfortable position that wouldn't cause his side to ache. On the floor beside the bed lay several letters. One was from his eldest daughter, Tefnut, who was about to have her first child. He planned to visit her and Isis, his youngest daughter, who was living with Tefnut. A few months ago Isis had nearly gotten her father killed through her selfish conduct, and the shame of it had forced the girl to see herself clearly for the first time. Isis wore her shame like a cloak of thorns, and Meren often worried about her.

Another letter was from Meren's brother, whom everyone called Ra. It consisted of a plea for Meren to rescue him from creditors, yet again. Ra had wagered a valuable field on his estate in a chariot race, which he lost. Without the field, his estate couldn't produce enough grain to support itself. The letter brimmed with protestations of reform, with promises of prompt repayment, and grand plans for future riches once his debts were paid. Meren didn't finish reading the letter. He had half a dozen similar ones; none had resulted in reform or repayment.

The sun had dropped low enough to shine into the windows, and Meren covered his eyes with his forearm. He was thinking about his brother when he felt his skin prickle, and he sensed another presence in the room. Without moving, Meren tensed his muscles and listened. He heard something brush against the sheers hanging from the frame around the bed, twisted and dropped to the floor while he groped for the dagger that always lay beneath the bed. As he moved he caught sight of a dark figure against the pale curtains and froze.

"Karoya!" Meren remained crouched on the floor, the dagger aimed at the Nubian before him while he fought the rush of sensation caused by alarm and battle readiness. Then he lowered his blade. "Damnation. Must you sneak into my bedchamber like that?"

"The Golden One commands the presence of the Eyes of Pharaoh."

Meren rose and dropped the dagger on the bed. "Just because you're the chief royal bodyguard doesn't mean you must go about frightening everyone the king wishes to see."

Stately, impassive, and as tall as an obelisk, Karoya ignored Meren's complaint. "The living Horus has sent a chariot for you." Turning on his heel, he left the bedchamber without waiting to see if Meren was behind him.

It was nearly sunset when Meren followed Karoya through antechambers and reception halls, the cavernous throne room, and more antechambers of the royal palace until he came to the king's suite. Rows of guards stretched to either side of the gilded doors through which Karoya vanished, and Meren waited there, studying the glazed tiles in the lotus frieze along the walls of the antechamber. Lamplight cast wavering shadows across the impassive faces of the guards. Meren nodded at the captain, a man known for his valor in battle. The captain saluted him and spoke quietly.

"The lord is well?"

"It was only one arrow, Yuf."

"We thank Amun for protecting you, lord."

Meren inclined his head, glancing at the others in Yuf's company. "Your concern honors me."

Suddenly the gilded doors swung wide, and a young woman swept through them. Clad in a shift and transparent pleated overrobe, she gleamed with electrum and precious stones. A braided wig framed her face with its pointed chin and gazelle's eyes. She moved with stately confidence, and her heavy jewels clicked together as she walked. She paused when she saw Meren, who bowed low before her.

"Ah, Lord Meren," she said in a low voice as a girl bearing a harp made of costly wood and ivory appeared behind her.

"Great royal wife, may you live forever in health and prosperity."

"You're better. Nebamun has driven out the fever demon that attacked you."

Meren kept his gaze fixed on the floor, his back bent. "I am unworthy of thy concern, majesty."

"Nonsense. Straighten up, my lord. I don't want my husband to hear I kept you in an uncomfortable position when you're not yet fully recovered."

Meren straightened and said, "All of Egypt knows the kindness of thy majesty."

Ankhesenamun waved her attendant away and walked across the chamber. "A word, my lord."

Meren reluctantly followed the queen. Ankhesenamun had never liked him. A follower of her father's heresy, she blamed Meren among others for advising the king to abandon the Aten and return to the old gods. More recently he'd foiled her attempt to replace Tutankhamun with a Hittite prince, and it had taken her a long time to convince her husband of her contrition.

Meren didn't believe in her reformation. He could see the same obsidian fire in her eyes that had burned in her father's. That black void of chaos had haunted him since Akhenaten had his father killed for refusing to conform to the heresy. Sometimes his dreams consisted solely of those eyes chasing him, tearing into his soul, ferreting out its deepest secrets, ravaging him until he longed for extinction. No, he didn't believe Akhenaten's favorite daughter had reformed. She was too much like him.

"How may I serve thy majesty?"

"It is a small thing, and yet a great one, my lord."

Ankhesenamun held a fan that she plied gently, sending a small breeze toward him that carried the scent of myrrh, cinnamon, and oil of lilies. Her bracelets clicked rhythmically, and the tension he'd felt ever since encountering the

queen faded with the mesmerizing scent and sound. Ankhesenamun's throaty whisper joined the motion of her fan and
the pleasing sound of her jewels.

"I've had much time to think, my lord. You and I have
been rowing in opposite directions for some time, but my
husband has spoken to me of your care of him, how you
guard him with your life. For that I'm grateful, and I regret
our past differences."

"Thy majesty is as generous as the goddess Isis. I am unworthy."

"No, Lord Meren. You were right not to trust me."

Meren's eyes widened, but he said nothing. The queen's
own eyes glittered with green malachite and black kohl, and
behind them flitted hints of grief and indefinable emotions
that twisted and writhed briefly, and then vanished.

"I was intolerant, and I was angry at having to abandon
all I knew in Horizon of the Aten to come here among
those who hated my father and therefore hated me. But,
slowly, I have come to understand the necessity." The fan
stopped, and Ankhesenamun slapped it against her palm,
giving Meren a smile he'd never seen before, one of teasing
mischief. "Besides, I like Memphis. So many colorful foreigners live here, and it's closer to the oases, which I love."

"I'm glad, majesty."

"So we must begin again, you and I."

Meren bowed. "Of course, majesty."

The queen turned to leave. "You don't believe me. No,
don't protest. I didn't expect you to. You will in time. A
good evening to you, my lord."

The little girl with the harp scurried after her mistress.
Meren raised one eyebrow and wondered what had brought
about the queen's new strategy. Ankhesenamun had never
been fond of compromise, conciliation, or forgiveness.

The daughter of Akhenaten and Nefertiti, she had grown up in Horizon of the Aten. Nefertiti had protected her daughters from the conflicts and intrigues that festered in the royal court, but in doing so she isolated them from all disagreement and contrary opinions. Ankhesenamun grew up listening to her father expound upon his beliefs. She still followed the precepts of his religion. Akhenaten had made her his favorite; Ankhesenamun had loved and believed in him without question. Unfortunately she had also absorbed his fanatical intolerance, and she deeply resented Tut-ankhamun and his ministers for leaving her father's ideal city and reconciling with the old gods, especially Amun. To her the priests of Amun, who had led the resistance against Akhenaten, were traitors, unbelievers, and eternal enemies.

Meren refused to believe that she'd changed so much in so short a time. He was prepared to believe, however, that she'd adapted to her new situation after her treachery had been thwarted, and waited for a more auspicious moment in which to assert herself. She must have a new advisor who'd convinced her that the way to power lay in changing her conduct. He would have to find out who this advisor was; he would bear watching, for the king's sake.

Karoya appeared and led Meren into the royal presence. The doors closed at his back, and Karoya disappeared into the shadow of one of the four painted columns that soared to the roof. At Meren's feet stretched a brilliant painting of a pool brimming with fish and water plants, and the whole room swam in light provided by alabaster lamps. At the opposite end, on a couch bearing gilded leather cushions, sat Tutankhamun, pharaoh of Egypt.

For a moment Meren held still, caught off guard by the fact that the king's flesh seemed to have turned to gold. The yellow metal was eternal; it never tarnished or succumbed to rust. The gods had flesh made of gold, and the king was the son of Amun by a mortal woman. It was the sign of immortality and divinity. Shimmering, eternal gold, flesh of the gods.

Tutankhamun moved, and the spell broke. Kneeling to touch his forehead to the floor, Meren chastised himself for falling prey to ignorant fancies. Of course the king was divine, the golden Horus incarnate. There was no need to imagine him literally turning to gold on earth.

"Come, Meren, and sit."

Meren joined him on the floor beside the couch. The king was holding a papyrus roll, and he'd been reading it by the light of half a dozen lamps, which accounted for the golden glow. Pharaoh had cast aside the weighty accoutrements of kings in favor of a simple kilt held by a belt with a buckle of openwork filigree red gold. On his right hand was a silver signet ring engraved with the royal cartouches. Heavy earrings lay on a table beside the couch along with a wine flagon and goblets of electrum. A servant appeared and poured wine. Tutankhamun clapped his hands, and Meren heard unseen attendants file out of the chamber. He glimpsed Karoya moving to close a door and stand beside it, his gaze as impassive as ever. They were given as much privacy as the king could ever expect.

Tutankhamun leaned against the high back of the couch, the papyrus still held loosely in one hand. "You're sailing tomorrow even though you're not fully recovered."

"I'm well, majesty."

"I'm not going to argue with you anymore. My physician has told me that forcing you to remain idle any longer would do little good."

"Thy majesty is wise."

"Wise enough to know you're up to something. You're going to Syene. Why?"

The king often knew what he was going to do before Meren told him. Ay, Meren, and the boy's other mentor, Horemheb, had trained the king to keep himself independently informed as a protection against anyone who might attempt to manipulate him. Still, it was disconcerting that Tutankhamun discovered things so quickly.

"I'm going to find Queen Nefertiti's chief bodyguard, Sebek."

"He's in Syene? You showed me old documents that recorded a gift of land in the Hare nome when he retired."

"But he's not there now," Meren said. "I suppose he must have traded the gift for a property in Syene. The cook's sister, Satet, told me about him. I talked to her frequently, hoping to spur her memory, and for once I was successful."

"And then she fell down a well," the king said.

"Yes, Golden One."

"An accident?"

"Majesty, there is no way to know."

Tutankhamun picked up the two goblets and handed one to Meren. The king took a sip of wine, then stared into the pool of dark liquid. His eyes were large, heavy-lidded, with thick lashes that often hid the sensitivity that made the burdens of a god-king heavy to bear. In this private moment he'd abandoned the stateliness that was so much a part of him, yet even now Meren felt the gravity and personal dignity that warred with the normal impulses of youth.

The king's cheeks hadn't lost all the roundness of youth. His lips had that lush fullness for which his mother, the great Queen Tiye, had been so famous. Even had he not been king the ladies of the court would have sought his favor, for he was wide of shoulder, lean from many hours on the practice field, and graceful in a way that would make him a formidable warrior in time. But those shadows were still there under his eyes, and he had a haunted air that worried Meren. As if to confirm his concern Tutankhamun turned abruptly, set down his goblet, and uttered a wordless sound of frustration and pain.

"When will this end—the killing, the treachery? Must I live my whole life looking over my shoulder? And how can I bear it, knowing that Nefertiti died at the hands of some faceless animal who sneaks and skulks and waits for an unguarded moment in which to strike?"

Tutankhamun whirled around to face Meren and spoke in a fierce whisper. "I want to be the one to find this murderer, to avenge my beloved second mother, but I can't. My majesty must sit in splendid idleness while others do what I should be doing. I fear that the queen's ka is suffering while I do nothing."

"That isn't true, majesty." Meren drew near the king. "All that I do is done by your command. I am thy majesty's eyes and ears." Meren lowered his voice. "And it is by thy wish that I will avenge the incomparable Queen Nefertiti, may her ka live forever."

Tutankhamun looked at him for a long time, his body tense, his gaze full of turmoil. At last he spoke through pale lips. "And what are you going to do now in my name?"

"Golden One, I must find someone who can link the steward Wah and the cook to the one who gave the order to kill her. Or I must find other proof such as a document that does the same thing." Meren hesitated, then went on. "I'm going to search for old records at Horizon of the Aten."

Tutankhamun winced, but said nothing. Meren disliked reminding the king of his former residence. Like Ankhesenamun, the king hated leaving Horizon of the Aten. He remembered no other home, and he had played among the date palms, acacias and incense trees, sunken gardens, ponds, and reflection pools that formed an idyllic playground for the royal children.

Meren understood how difficult it had been for pharaoh to leave Horizon of the Aten, but Tutankhamun had accepted that in order to bring peace to Egypt he had to heal the schism created by Akhenaten. One of the most important steps toward that goal had been to move the capital of Egypt back to the great city of Memphis where it had been for millennia. By making such public gestures pharaoh reassured his people that Maat, order and rightness of existence, had returned to Egypt.

The king looked away and whispered. "I wish I could go with you."

"Majesty . . ."

The king inhaled sharply and lifted his shoulders. Meren watched the boy's expression change. Personal grief vanished beneath the distant visage of the ruler of an empire.

At last the king spoke. "Very well. It's best you make a quiet detour on the way to somewhere else. A trip with Horizon of the Aten as its only destination would attract speculation."

"Yes, Golden One."

"I'm glad Anath is going with you."

Meren turned to look at the king. "The Eyes of Babylon is the source of thy majesty's knowledge."

"Of course." Tutankhamun smiled at him. "You taught me well, Meren. I'd know if you purchased a new horse or caught an ague."

He took another sip of wine. "Enough of this misery. On to another trouble. Burnaburiash of Babylon has sent me a letter complaining that I received emissaries from the king of Assyria. He's furious that I saw them when they're his vassals. He says they should communicate with me through him. Anath told me the old devil's health isn't good, and he's becoming possessed with dread of rivals. She recommends that I assuage his fearfulness so he won't be tempted to seek out a Hittite alliance."

"The Eyes of Babylon knows the old king well, majesty. I've never had cause to regret following her advice."

Setting his wine down, Tutankhamun nodded. A spasm of pain crossed his face. "I want this evil business over with, Meren. Find out who caused Nefertiti's death, or I think I shall go mad with the uncertainty."

"I won't stop looking until I know the truth." Meren bowed from his sitting position. "I swear by all the gods, majesty."

The king smiled at him, but the smile faded as his gaze dropped to the place where the arrow had entered Meren's body. Meren looked away, wishing he didn't remember what had caused the wound. A few weeks ago Nefertiti's murderer had launched a campaign to disgrace Meren and implicate him in an attempt on Tutankhamun's life. He'd been trying to prove his innocence to pharaoh when an assassin in the service of the evil one had shot an arrow. The man's aim had been off, or the arrow would have killed the king instead of Meren.

"If you hadn't grabbed me and taken that arrow, I'd be dead," the king said. His eyes brightened with unshed tears. "I'll never forget that."

"I did no more than any of thy majesty's servants would."

Tutankhamun shook his head gently. "I must find a way to show my gratitude." He raised his hand to prevent Meren from speaking. "No more of your protests."

"Yes, majesty."

The king's gaze fell to the papyrus he'd allowed to fall beside him on the couch. Picking it up, he unrolled it to reveal a text with painted decorations. Meren saw the Aten disk, and his heart banged against his ribs and he felt light-headed. Setting his wine on the floor, he covered his scar with his hand. He always wore an armband or bracelet over it, but the gesture was unthinking. Tutankhamun saw the movement and frowned. Regret was plain in his expression.

"Akhenaten gave this to me a few months before he died. It's in his hand, a copy of his Hymn to the Aten."

Meren nodded and made himself drop the hand that covered the old brand. Tutankhamun had few in whom he could confide his real feelings about his family. He wouldn't punish the boy for Akhenaten's transgressions.

Tutankhamun was gazing at the lines of the hymn. "It's beautiful, what he says about all people being creatures of the sun god, how he made them diverse in speech, habits, and color. The Aten makes the Nile in Egypt and rain in other lands; his rays make the fields grow, the seasons pass; and he sheds light on all the world."

"Indeed, Golden One. Thy brother the king was divine in his writings."

Meren didn't add that Akhenaten had appropriated all communication with the Aten to himself. Everyone else had to worship the king, because only Akhenaten knew his father, the sun. The Aten created the cosmos, but after that, the sun disk must have forgotten about it, because the rest was left to Akhenaten. Only he knew his father's thoughts and wishes, and he interpreted them for everyone else. All worship was directed to the Aten, and to his son, Akhenaten. The heretic even had priests in charge of worshipping himself. Over and over Akhenaten stressed that the bounty of

Egypt and its well-being depended upon him and the Aten only.

Meren remembered the other hymns and the inscriptions dictated by Akhenaten to be carved in his courtiers' tombs. Paeans to himself, they were. Akhenaten was the living disk, unequaled, and there was no other. The king, the sun, was the source of all power, and none could escape his dominion. He remembered the tomb reliefs, in which everyone worshipped Akhenaten, and Akhenaten worshipped the Aten.

Something else stirred in Meren's memory, something important, but it vanished when the king sighed and released one end of the papyrus. It rolled shut.

"Take care on this journey, Meren. Horizon of the Aten is now a place of misfortune, I think."

Pain lanced into Meren's heart as the king's eyes became glassy with unshed tears. "Remember what they did to my brother's body."

"I do, majesty."

Rabid with lust for vengeance, the heretic's enemies had tried to destroy his soul and that of Nefertiti by destroying their mummified bodies. They hadn't succeeded in destroying the bodies completely, but Meren didn't think that mattered. When Akhenaten died and his ka journeyed to the netherworld, he faced the judgment of the very gods he tried to destroy. Meren shivered as he contemplated Akhenaten's fate.

Absolute annihilation. His soul must have been obliterated. Meren tried to imagine the absence of existence, the nothingness, of an erased ka. It was as if he stood on the brink of a cliff looking over the edge into an endless void. This was surely Akhenaten's fate. Meren only hoped it had not been Nefertiti's. They looked at each other, he and pharaoh. This unspoken fear lay between them, binding them, driving them. He waited for the king to speak of it, but Tutankhamun had done with exposing his innermost secrets. The boy disliked making himself vulnerable, even to Meren in whom he confided much. He almost started when Tutankhamun touched his arm gently.

"My majesty wishes you to guard yourself well on this journey, Meren," said the king.

Meren smiled. "Thy majesty may be correct that the gods look with ill favor upon those who go to Horizon of the Aten. But I won't be there long, and I'll have Anath to protect me."

"Good. Anath is worth an entire company of charioteers. There is no other woman like her."

Chapter 4

On the evening of the day his father sailed for Horizon of the Aten, Kysen dallied on a wharf near the Caverns. He heard the noise of hammers coming across the river. Someone was working at the naval docks by torchlight.

At the moment he was disguised as Nen, a scribe fallen on hard times who dealt in other people's secrets. Nen sold information for valuable goods—metals, expensive woods or stones such as malachite and lapis lazuli. Nen lived in the dark world of thieves, corrupt government officials, whores, and murderers. He was supposed to be the sixth son of the assistant to the steward of a minor noble. From a family with numerous children, he had little wealth, but a taste for luxuries, and he didn't care how he acquired them. In the Caverns he was known for his clever heart and dislike of hard labor.

Nen dressed in a kilt with slightly tattered edges and a plain leather belt that had been mended in several places. His wig was one he'd gotten secondhand. It fit with the character he sought to portray. Once the wig had been finely plaited, and its tresses were cut short in back and were longer in front. Now the wig looked worn, and some of the locks were coming loose from the net of threads to which they were attached. Nevertheless, it was surely the cast-off head-dress of a nobleman.

Secure in his disguise Kysen strolled down the Street of the Ibex and into the foreign quarter. The buildings in this area had been built tightly against each other in long, ir-regular rows, scarcely big enough for two people to squeeze by. The roads were dusty and littered with refuse and slops. More than once he had to dodge a cloud of dust from the broom of a homeowner or shopkeeper who used the street as a waste receptacle.

He shouldered through a group of sailors speaking one of the languages of the Asiatics outside a beer tavern, and turned down a passageway that led to an alley. He dodged an inebriated Syrian merchant who stumbled out of a house and tried to vomit, then lurched back inside. The door slammed, and Kysen was alone. He remained motionless, waiting. Soon other figures appeared in the passageway. One of them flitted up to him.

"We're all here, lord."

"Excellent, Reia. Five of us should be enough to deal with one fat merchant, don't you think?"

"Yes, lord."

Reia smiled at him. One of Meren's most trusted char-ioteers, he ranked highest after Abu. Reia had risen through the ranks of the royal bodyguard. His father was a physi-cian's assistant, not a nobleman, and Kysen felt more at ease with him than with the charioteers who came from aristo-cratic families. Competition to become one of the com-pany serving the Eyes and Ears of Pharaoh was fierce, but

Meren selected men by their character and skill as well as their lineage.

Almost as tall as a Nubian, with large hands and a severe expression, Reia was fanatically loyal to Meren, grateful to him for taking a chance on him despite his lack of high rank. Kysen knew how Reia felt. To be a commoner cast among noblemen was to be a duck swimming with crocodiles. He himself had been born to a carpenter who worked on the royal tombs but was adopted by Meren. He too loved Meren for his kindness and generosity, for he'd saved Kysen from his real father, Pawero. Kysen had taken beatings for any misfortune that befell Pawero. Eleven years ago, when Kysen was eight, Meren had purchased him from the carpenter. Since then he'd learned to be a nobleman, a role he was sure he'd never completely master.

Turning his attention back to the charioteers, he addressed Reia. "Very well. We'll go in pairs and singly so as not to be too conspicuous. I've found out that our fat merchant Dilalu is going to visit the Divine Lotus, which we all remember well. According to my informant, Dilalu will meet with Ese, although I can't imagine that lady enjoying his company."

"She owns the Divine Lotus," Reia said. "Perhaps she's being hospitable."

"Only if it suits her interests," Kysen said.

"Indeed, Lord."

With a salute, Reia and the others disappeared, and Kysen continued on his way. A short walk down a road at the edge of the foreign district brought him to his destination. He mounted the steps that led to the door and shoved it open to reveal a crowded central chamber designed to imitate a Greek villa. The great hall had a circular central hearth around which many customers had gathered against the chill of the evening.

Ese had decorated the place with frescoes of women in Greek dress with tight bodices that bared their breasts, flounced skirts, and gold rosette earrings. Geometric friezes bordered the scenes—spirals, zigzags, and stripes. By designing her tavern after a Greek megaron Ese attracted Egyptian customers to an exotic place, and foreign ones were drawn by the novelty of the serving maids, dancers, and hostesses dressed in the fashions displayed in the frescoes.

Walking over to a table laden with wine and beer jars, Kysen traded a small faience amulet on a string of shell beads for a jar of beer with a strainer. Holding it and a ceramic cup he wandered over to a corner and stood drinking and watching from the shadows. On mats and cushions throughout the room rested Greeks from Crete and Cyprus, nomads from the eastern desert, a wealthy trader from Corinth, and sailors from ships as far away as Rhodes and Tyre. The shadows far from the hearth provided lurking places for every kind of charlatan and predator attracted to the capital of a mighty empire. Pirates, corrupt government officials, and ordinary villains abounded. Kysen wasn't looking for any of these; he was searching for Dilalu, the weapons merchant.

Inquiries into the man's past had revealed that Dilalu had sold horses to Queen Nefertiti. Delving further, Meren's agents found that while profiting from this royal patronage Dilalu had been busy arranging to sell scimitars, bows, arrows, daggers, and lances to rebellious Egyptian vassals in Canaan. Among these had been Aziru of Amurru, a troublemaker who defied the pharaoh Akhenaten and pledged his loyalty to the king of the Hittites.

Before she died, Nefertiti had ordered her agents to find

whoever was supplying the vassals with weapons and destroy
him. So Dilalu had had a good reason to want the queen
dead. With her gone he could ply his trade throughout Canaan,
Syria, and Palestine, making himself rich on the interminable
disputes of Egyptian vassals.

Kysen hadn't taken more than a few sips of his beer when
he saw Reia come in with another charioteer. A third man
appeared shortly afterward, followed by a fourth. He was
halfway finished with the jar, however, before Dilalu strode
into the tavern holding his pet cat clutched to his chest like
a treasure. Dilalu never went anywhere without his pet cat,
a corpulent tabby with a nasty disposition and a flat head.

The weapons merchant had a gait like a pyramid block
with legs. He walked with his chin jutting out and his el-
bows likewise, and Kysen knew that when he came close to
the man he'd smell of expensive unguents. The merchant's
soft skin was oiled, as was his hair, which he wore in tight
curls and which hung above his shoulders. He'd recently
shaved his beard so that his cheeks and chin were a lighter
brown than the rest of his face.

Kysen caught Reia's eye and nodded in the merchant's direction. Reia eased over to lounge near Dilalu while the others circled at a distance. Oblivious to their presence, Dilalu
chatted with Ese's assistant, a woman with long, red-tinted
hair. Kysen knew Ese. Although the Divine Lotus catered to
the physical comfort of its guests—whether it be thirst, entertainment, or lust—Ese seldom bestowed her personal favor
upon a customer. If she did so, it was for an enormous fee.
She detested most men, and Kysen was sure she would never
consider entertaining the portly and slimy Dilalu. No, Dilalu was visiting Ese for some more nefarious reason. Pos-
sibly he wanted her to introduce him to agents of vassal
princes in need of weapons. Whatever the case, Ese would

probably make him wait to see her, thus asserting her importance and command.

Near the hearth musicians struck up a tune with a heavy drumbeat, and three women began to dance. As patrons surged toward the center of the room to see the performance Dilalu followed his hostess toward the rear, through a stairwell and out a door. Kysen followed, waited at the door until he saw the woman leave her guest alone in a garden court, and then slipped outside.

Dilalu had wandered to a reflection pool in the court and was trying to keep his cat from leaping at some ducks swimming there. He wore a fine wool robe that must have taken a flock of sheep to make. It was yellow, blue, and red with a fringe spangled with gold thread. While he wrestled with the cat his sandals slipped on the tiles that bordered the pool.

Dilalu admonished his cat. "Behave yourself, Enlil."

He moved away from the water to stand beside a tall lamp stand, nearly knocking it over and causing the flame to flutter.

Behind the merchant Kysen remained in the black shadow of a date palm as the cat squirmed and clawed. Dilalu yelped, and twisted around, his gaze finding Kysen at last. He squinted, then smiled.

"Mistress Ese, at last. My eternal thanks for agreeing to help me, for I seem to have attracted too much attention from those in authority, that cursed Lord Meren, especially. I need your help in leaving the city without being noticed." When Kysen didn't answer, Dilalu moved nearer and squinted harder. "Mistress Ese?"

"Greetings, merchant," Kysen said.

Dilalu turned around, saw Kysen, and lifted one eyebrow. "Who are you? Don't I know you?"

"I want to speak to you."

When Kysen made no threatening moves, the merchant scowled at him and stroked Enlil.

"I'm busy, youth. I await Mistress Ese."

Kysen glanced around the courtyard and spotted Reia, who nodded. The other charioteers were already moving around the garden to surround their quarry.

"Mistress Ese isn't coming," Kysen said.

Alarmed, Dilalu backed away, his eyes flitting from one man to another. He opened his mouth and emitted a high scream.

"Shut up!" Kysen clamped a hand over Dilalu's mouth. The cat Enlil growled and raked his arm with sharp claws. Kysen cursed and withdrew his hand.

"Helphelphelphelphelp!"

Luckily the music, drums, and clapping that accompanied the dancers in the tavern made it impossible to hear Dilalu. The merchant scurried away from Kysen, his cat under one arm, dodging Reia and the other charioteers. Kysen ran after him, leaping over a corner of the reflection pool. He landed in front of Dilalu, who shrieked and threw the cat at him. Enlil yowled and bounced off Kysen's chest, hit the ground, and became a ball of claws and teeth. As the drums and music grew even louder, Kysen sprang backward out of his reach and whirled around at the sharp clang of metal. Half a dozen men had appeared without warning. Armed with scimitars and swords, they rushed the charioteers. Kysen had come armed only with a dagger. He drew it as Reia dispatched an attacker and pounced on another.

Dilalu took advantage of the distraction to maneuver around Kysen and race along the edge of the pool. Kysen ran after him and caught Dilalu's robe. The merchant tripped over the fringe on his gown and fell to his knees. Kysen stooped, intending to grab the neck of the robe, but something heavy hit him from behind, and his knees buckled. Before he could defend himself another blow glanced off the back of his head. He fell face forward in the water, and someone jumped on him and shoved his head under; Kysen breathed in water and struggled frantically.

As suddenly as he'd been shoved under the water he was released. He came up choking and sputtering. Water erupted from his nose and mouth, and he sucked in air.

"You idiot, that's him!" said a harsh, foreign-accented voice. "Bring him, quickly."

Someone grabbed Kysen's wig. It came off, and he heard a curse. Before he could gather enough strength to resist he was bashed in the head again and slung over a shoulder. Dazed, Kysen felt his stomach try to fall into his throat. He was moving. Then, without warning, the ground slammed into him. Around him he heard the noise of battle, then shouts and the pounding of retreating feet. He made swimming motions in the dirt, and gathered his legs beneath him. His vision cleared, and he was able to roll over.

Someone was standing over him. Kysen's hand went to the dagger sheath at his side. It was empty; he'd dropped his dagger when he'd been hit.

"It's me, lord."

"Reia." Kysen blinked up at the charioteer. "What happened?"

Reia helped him stand. "You took a blow to the head, lord."

Kysen shoved his wet hair back from his face. He felt his skull and found a bump that felt like it was the size of a crocodile's egg. Mud streaked his arms, legs, and face.

"Where did those men come from? I thought Dilalu was alone."

"So did I," Reia said as he sheathed his sword.

Kysen looked around the garden court. "They're all gone?"

"Yes, lord."

"Even Dilalu."

Reia nodded, handing Kysen his dagger. "When we stopped them from dragging you off, they retreated."

"Strange," Kysen said as he wiped the blade on his kilt. "Why would they try to abduct me in the middle of rescuing Dilalu?"

Reia was scowling, deep in thought. "Remember what the merchant said?"

"No, I don't. Not with this knot on my head." Kysen winced.

"He yelled at his men. He said 'you idiot, that's him.' It seemed to me that he recognized you. In fact, it seemed to me that he expected to find you here. Hoped to find you. The porter and the guards who are usually on duty at the gates over there vanished once Dilalu began to speak to you."

"You think he planned to abduct me? Why?"

"I don't know, lord. Perhaps Dilalu is in league with the killer sought by Lord Meren. But I may be wrong. Perhaps he was telling the truth and simply wished help in leaving because you've made him wary. But with all the misfortunes that have beset your father lately, I don't wish to stand here speculating."

"Damnation." Kysen threw up his hands. "Even that cursed cat got away."

Reia pointed at Kysen's scratched arm. "Cats are usually good luck, but that one must be possessed by a fiend."

"Curse it, Reia, I've bungled everything. Now we'll have to root Dilalu out of his house before he flees the city. Come on."

Kysen took several steps and swayed as the world tilted. Reia and another charioteer caught him.

"Dilalu can wait. I'm taking you back to Golden House so that Nebamun can tend to you."

"Just give me a moment, and I'll be fine," Kysen said.

Reia and another charioteer grasped his arms, and Kysen found himself being steered out of the garden court.

"We're going home, lord. I can't be sure you're the hunter any longer. You may be the prey. Besides, if I allowed you to continue in your condition, Lord Meren would see me flayed and fed to the king's lions."

"I'm not leaving before I talk to Ese!"

"Lord Meren charged me with protecting you before he left. I would greatly dislike being forced to throw you over my shoulder in the manner of your attacker."

"Damn you, Reia, I'll remember this."

"Of that I'm certain, Lord Kysen."

Chapter 5

Meren stood on the deck of *Wings of Horus*. The cloak of early morning wrapped him in a chilly embrace, and he listened to the water lap against the sides of this, his fastest ship. Long, sleek, black, it had covered the distance between Memphis and Horizon of the Aten more quickly than he would have wished. Three days after embarking he was waiting for the sun—Ra, not the Aten—to burst upon the eastern horizon and reveal Akhenaten's capital.

He hadn't wanted to return again to this skeleton of a city, the site of his torment. For most of the seventeen long years of his rule, Akhenaten and his government had lodged here. Akhenaten had chosen a pristine site for his new capital, a place where the eastern desert cliffs retreated from the Nile valley and formed a backdrop of crescent-shaped cream-colored rock. Perched on this barren plain, the city had baked in the relentless rays of the Aten and the fanatic gaze of the god's son, Akhenaten. Without the shade provided by trees and vegetation, life had been miserable at first. Everyone except Akhenaten had welcomed the arrival of an army of gardeners with seedlings and trees from the old capital. Later, when Akhenaten's sun temples were completed, worship in sunlight rather than the coolness of a sacred shrine added to the city's discomfort.

Pharaoh had been oblivious to everyone's suffering, but the heat had been the least part of Meren's difficulties. He'd been so young, eighteen, when his father defied Akhenaten and died for his crime. Sending his beloved wife and daughters away from Horizon of the Aten had been a precaution, one of which Meren had been glad the day the king's soldiers had come for him. He'd been eating his morning meal at home when he heard a crash, and the porter came running to tell him—what? The poor man couldn't speak. Meren could see him now, his mouth working noiselessly, his eyes bulging with fear. And behind him five massive Nubian soldiers.

Meren had promised himself not to succumb to miserable recollections. He hugged himself and began to pace down the length of the ship. It was Horizon of the Aten, this near-deserted, decaying carcass of a city that had once been so terrifyingly beautiful. Horizon of the Aten did this to him.

Ra, lord of the heavens, rose over the city. Meren went to the railing and looked out, past the docks that had so recently brimmed with the spoils of the empire, over the rooftops of the storehouses, and glimpsed the top of the ceremonial center called the Great Palace. There, in a throne room made brilliant with painted tiles and vast quantities of gold and electrum, Akhenaten had received his ministers and given audience to foreign ambassadors—when he wasn't at the Great Aten Temple.

The monumental buildings of stone and brick remained; only their valuable metal and wood fittings had been taken away. But their creator, the man whose presence filled them with the light of fanaticism and the bustle of royal business, was gone, and no one else wanted to live here. Oh, a few priests stayed to keep up the pretense of tending the royal tombs and make offerings to the kas of the dead king and his family. Across the river small farms thrived as they had before Akhenaten ever thought of living here. A few people traded on the docks. But the tens of thousands of royal officials, servants, the master craftsmen, the laborers and their families, the great freighters full of grain, wood, flax, and the spoils of the empire had vanished, never to return.

Meren dragged his gaze away and wondered where Anath was. Her smaller yacht had followed *Wings of Horus* up the river, but she spent each day with him and regaled him with tales of her exploits among the Asiatics. Anath could make the fiercest outlaw chief seem ridiculous with her biting and perceptive observations. This talent for detailed scrutiny made her an extremely valuable royal agent. She had also learned to use magic to further her aims, and Meren feared she employed it too freely in manipulating people. It was all done, according to Anath, for the good of pharaoh and Egypt.

What surprised him, though, was how she made him laugh, even at himself. She was an amazing woman to have retained her humor after being exiled among the Asiatics for so long. Meren would have suffered terribly without being able to see the Nile every day. However, Anath had one weakness—her animals. Luckily she hadn't brought all of them with her. The one she had was more than enough.

"You're glowering like an underworld fiend."

Meren started and whirled around to find Anath standing a few paces away, her head cocked to the side, hands on her hips.

"Damnation, Anath, where did you come from?"

"I came aboard moments ago," she said as she joined him. "You would have noticed if you hadn't been transfixed by the sunrise. Where were your thoughts, Meren?"

Meren moved away from her, avoiding her speculative gaze. "I was thinking about your recommendation that we begin searching at the Riverside Palace."

He went to the awning attached to the deckhouse where his cook was laying out a meal. A small kitchen boat followed *Wings of Horus* with supplies and the cook and his assistants. He sat on a woven mat and drank water while the cook filled a bowl with roasted goose. Anath strolled over, sat down, and took another bowl.

Meren lifted a drumstick and was about to bite into it when he thought of something. "Cook, this isn't that evil goose of old Satet's, is it?"

"No, lord. Beauty still lives. It would be bad luck to kill that old pestilence. Lady Bener gave orders that Beauty was to be kept as a pet just as Satet intended."

Anath was looking out at the city. "I remember how green this place used to be."

"Everyone took what could be uprooted back to Memphis," Meren said as he tore off a piece of flatbread. "And the rest, well, there aren't enough people to keep a tenth part of the gardens. They aren't needed anyway."

They ate in silence, steadily, for it was nearly time to leave for the city. Meren's sailors and charioteers were busy unloading chariots and horses from the ship, and activity went on all around them.

Meren forced himself to finish the food set before him, not wanting to risk being scolded by the cook. Then he washed his hands, gave the cook a nod of approval, and stood. Anath was watching Abu supervise the hitching of

Meren's thoroughbreds to his chariot. Nearby stood Meren's three scribes, Kenro, Dedi, and Bekenamun, who was called Bek. They would supervise the search for documents while Meren and Anath explored the city looking for other likely repositories.

"Dedi, your team will begin at the magazines at the King's House," he said as he walked down the gangplank. "Bek will go to the office of records and tithes, and Kenro, you search the office of the correspondence of pharaoh. That's where you're more likely to find the foreign documents you're so good at translating."

The various parties set off, and Meren got into his chariot. Anath was standing with his thoroughbreds, Wind Chaser and Star Chaser. She murmured softly to Wind and brushed her cheek against his soft nose. Meren was about to tell her it was time to go when something jumped into the chariot with him. He gasped and looked down at the floor of the vehicle to find that Anath's cat, Khufu, had decided to join him.

Meren scowled at the creature, but Khufu ignored him and calmly began to lick one of his paws. Khufu was named after the mighty pharaoh who built the Great Pyramid, but he reminded Meren of Tcha, a greasy, illiterate denizen of the Caverns. The cat was striped gray, white, and black, and built like a compact baboon. He was disfigured from his many battles with dogs, monkeys, other cats, and anything else that moved. His ears were tattered, his face scarred, and one of his eyelids drooped. Khufu lived to fight, and the only creature he didn't try to coerce was his mistress.

"Go away, Khufu."

The cat glanced up at him, then dropped into a reclining position.

Setting his jaw, Meren gathered the reins. "Come, Anath, we're wasting time."

Anath got into the chariot and took the reins from him. "I've been cooped up on a ship too long. Driving will do me good."

Slapping the reins on the horses' backs, she walked them across the waterfront and turned the chariot onto the Royal Road. Meren kept quiet as they slowed and then stopped. They were beside the Mansion of the Aten, Akhenaten's royal chapel for the worship of his god. A few hundred yards beyond lay the bridge that Akhenaten had built from the Great Palace to the King's House, the place where pharaoh had conducted his daily business.

The Royal Road stretched into the distance, the fencing that had once kept pedestrians safe from passing chariots now slowly decaying. Here in the central city lay most of the royal departments and the Aten temples. To the north and south stood residential areas along with the estates of master craftsmen such as the great sculptor, Thutmose. Farther north lay smaller palaces, and finally, the enormous Riverside Palace, the fortified private residence of pharaoh and his family.

As they surveyed the city, the north breeze picked up. Debris blew over the Royal Road while here and there doors that hadn't been removed and taken away slammed back and forth on their hinges. At their feet Khufu gave a low growl and curled himself around Anath's ankles, and his mistress shivered.

Meren's gaze skimmed across the Royal Bridge and lighted on the Great Palace, the formal setting for Akhenaten's grandeur. Inside, surrounded by lofty columned halls, small courts, and monuments, lay the vast courtyard. Around its perimeter stood colossal statues of the heretic, each a ghastly distortion—splayed hips, emaciated shoulders, brooding, slanted eyes painted a glittering, brittle black. All the brilliantly painted and glazed tiles, the lush scenes of vegetation and wildlife that made the small courts and halls so beautiful, couldn't erase the bizarre impression of those colossi.

"Do you know what I remember about this place?" Anath asked quietly.

"What?"

"The disjunction between the beauty of it and the fear that was my enduring companion."

Meren darted a look at her, surprised that she would echo his innermost feelings. "Yes."

A look of pain passed over her features, then she shook herself as if to rid herself of bad memories. "Such symmetry, the balance between the Great Palace on one side of the Royal Road and the King's House on the other, the soaring reed-bundle columns in the Great Aten Temple, all of it so new and fresh. So unlike the old cities."

"We were never afraid in the old cities," Meren said to himself as he gazed at the King's House. To the east of it, among the myriad government offices, lay the guardhouse where he'd been tortured. He could still smell the place, the stench of old sweat, his own waste, and fear. His face set in an expressionless mask, Meren said, "Drive on. We're losing time."

Coming out of her own reverie, Anath slapped the reins once more, and they trotted down the Royal Road in the ruts made from the passage of the heretic's royal chariot. As if by mutual consent they refrained from talking about anything but their search for documents that could reveal a motive for killing Nefertiti. They drove far to the north, to the point where the high desert cliffs marched down to the Nile valley. Here Akhenaten had built the Riverside Palace, a vast complex with its own storehouses, grain magazines, and barracks, the whole of which was surrounded by battlements. They had no reason to search the cattle biers, the stables, or the kitchens, but Anath remembered the half dozen rooms in a building, between the palace and the fortified walls, where records were kept.

They left the horses tethered in the shade of a colonnade and entered the structure that had once served as an office for the king's steward. They stood in a large room, the roof of which was supported by four painted columns on stone bases. Strewn about the room were pieces of papyrus, broken shelves, and piles of ostraca, the pottery shards and limestone flakes that served as note tablets. Sand was beginning to form small drifts on the floor. In a few years it would completely obscure the whitewashed packed earth. In a few more this building and most of the others in the city would be choked with the encroaching desert.

"I'll start in the secretary's room," Anath said, and she disappeared through a doorway with Khufu strolling after her.

Meren sighed and began to search through a pile of ostraca with little hope of finding anything important. Why had he allowed Anath to persuade him to come here? He should have gone straight to Syene while his men and Anath searched Horizon of the Aten. For his part, all he seemed to do was sink into a morass of nightmarish memories that left the taste of blood in his mouth and the smell of death in his nostrils.

It took some while to sort through the contents of the steward's office. Anath surprised him with her diligence. She returned from the secretary's room with an armload of discarded papyri, which she dumped at his feet.

"I'll be back," she said as she sped across to the doorway opposite the one she'd first taken.

The morning passed in this manner, with Anath speeding around the palace offices, ducking into corners, and digging through piles of rubbish. She would dump documents and ostraca in front of Meren with orders that he pay particular attention to this text or that, then rush off in another direction. By midday she was almost finished and had settled herself on the floor beside Meren. Her fingers traced lines of cursive hieroglyphs, muttering imprecations against scribes with sloppy penmanship, and tossing useless documents in every direction.

Meren was reading a list of recipients of the Gold of Honor when Anath drew in a sharp breath. "Meren, look at this." She handed him a fragment of papyrus, one of many that had been left behind because oil from a lamp had spilled on them. It was stained but readable.

"It's from the queen," Meren said. He glanced at the date. "She wrote this about a month before she died."

Anath pointed to a line. "See what she says of Prince Usermontu."

Meren read the text aloud. ". . . the appointment of Prince Usermontu. He has diverted the supplies intended for pharaoh's garrison at the port of Sumur in the land of the Asiatics. The king's soldiers go without grain, and I will not countenance it. There is no reward . . ." Meren tried to read further, but the ink had spread and blurred. "I remember now. The queen was furious with Prince Usermontu, but she didn't tell me her reasons."

"He was diverting supplies to himself, stealing from the army," Anath said. "And she found out."

Meren nodded. "I remember her summoning Usermontu. I had come to deliver documents for Ay, and she kicked him out of the palace. Grabbed a spear from one of the guards and poked his arse all the way from the audience chamber to the pylon gates."

"Ha! I wish I'd seen that. Usermontu is a greedy reptile."

Narrowing his eyes, Meren studied the letter fragment. "There are many greedy servants of the king, but few angered her like Usermontu did. There must have been something more behind her anger."

"Perhaps his stealing caused deaths in Sumur. If the men weren't paid, they might desert and go home, leaving the outpost undefended."

"True."

Meren set the fragment aside, and they continued their search until the sun was low in the sky. By then they'd finished going through everything, and had come up with nothing else. A servant had brought roast swan, pelican eggs, date bread, and pomegranate wine at midday, but now Meren was hungry again, and his mood black.

"You're scowling again." Anath rose and dusted off her hands.

Meren threw a limestone flake on the pile that reached to his knees and got up as well. "This was a waste of time."

"I swear by Ishtar and Baal, Meren, you're miserable company."

"I'm not here to entertain you, Mistress Anath. We're running out of time. Soon now the evil one will realize I've returned to the search for Nefertiti's murderer, and the killing will begin again, if it hasn't already. Remember Satet."

Anath stalked over to him. "You don't have to remind me of our peril, Meren. I've risked bringing myself to the attention of this killer to help you."

"Thank you!" Meren's voice rose, so tense was he with frustration.

Planting her feet apart, Anath stuck her face close to his. "Thanks like that should come from an enemy, damn you."

"All we've found is one fragment telling of Usermontu's cheating and useless ration lists," Meren said, leaning over Anath and staring into her bright, uptilted eyes. "The whole search has been useless."

"You don't know that!"

"It's bound to be," Meren snapped. "The important records went back to Memphis." He turned his back on Anath, kicked aside a stack of papyrus scraps, and headed outside.

Before he got to the doorway Anath caught his arm and swung him around. Few dared to grab Lord Meren, Friend of the King, so her touch caught him off guard, and he jerked around, knocking her off balance. Anath cried out as she fell backward, but Meren caught her and pulled her upright. She let out a sound of irritation and shoved him, hard. Meren hit a wall, and his head banged against it. Pain exploded in his skull.

"Curse it, woman!" He lunged for her, grabbed her by the arms and shook her. "I'm not staying here any longer. Do you hear?"

Anath's hair swirled around her face. She shook it away from her eyes and glared at him. Meren was already regretting his loss of temper even while he found himself holding on to Anath. Her skin was smooth, as if she bathed in oil rather than water, and he could feel her body's tension, hear it in her rapid breathing. Her gaze lifted to his, and something dark stirred there.

Seldom had Meren allowed himself the luxury of giving free rein to lust. His life depended upon guarding his appetites lest they be used against him. Anath had been forced to do the same; he could see it in her eyes. Beyond the superficial slaking of lust lay the domain of love and desire, but that domain was ruled by trust. And trust was more precious than all the gold in pharaoh's mines, more rare than the black iron of the Hittites.

Anath whispered to him, "I have been too long among strangers, Meren."

"I also, Eyes of Babylon."

Her hand came up, and he held still while her fingertips traced the line of his jaw. "I have seen ancient pain come alive in you. What they did to you lives on in your ka, as timeless as the netherworld. Such pain forces you to be a stranger to all."

Meren closed his eyes, afraid she would see how close to the truth she'd come. He felt her fingertips on his lips. Blinded by pain and need, he took her mouth in his.

Chapter 6

Surrounded by scrolls and scraps of papyrus, document cases and chests, Kysen sat on the floor of his father's office beside the chair Meren occupied while conducting business. By now his father should be in Horizon of the Aten. Arching his back, Kysen yawned. He'd started out in the chair, but reading page after page of notes and culling through copies of government ration records made him sleepy.

He was angry with Reia for making him come home last night, and even angrier with himself for having lost Dilalu's trail. He'd sent men after the weapons trader, but the man wasn't at his home. They'd searched the docks and the foreign quarters in as unobtrusive a manner as possible, with no success. Dilalu had vanished.

Kysen had decided to review once again the information they'd gathered. During his enforced rest Meren had made notes on who might have had the opportunity and power to murder Nefertiti. Kysen dropped the papyrus containing Meren's notations on Dilalu and other suspects. Meren had continued to receive information from the agents he'd sent in search of old servants and courtiers of the queen. Using his own resources, Ese and the Greek pirate Othrys, Kysen had located almost a dozen former servants.

Yamen, the army officer they'd suspected, was dead. Meren had been on the verge of contacting the merchant Zulaya when he'd been wounded. The Greek pirate Othrys had suggested they investigate these two men, saying they had the power and daring to bring about a queen's murder.

Meren was of the opinion that even if one of these men was guilty, the ultimate responsibility for Nefertiti's death— indeed, for all that had happened during this investigation— lay with someone at the court. For months he'd pondered the question of who might have wanted the queen dead. A rival? The magnificent Nefertiti had no rivals, not even the minor queens and concubines of Akhenaten's household. Akhenaten's only love had been the great royal wife.

Although Meren could think of few women who might want to kill the queen, there might have been men who wished to do so. During her last years, Nefertiti had thwarted the ambitions of a number of parvenus. These men, whether from the aristocracy or not, had been of no consequence until they caught Akhenaten's eye. Usually they'd gained favor by impressing pharaoh with their fervor for the sun disk, their skill in ferreting out temple riches hidden by the old priesthood, or they ran royal departments without causing any work for the king.

One of these was Lord Pendua. He'd been a nonentity at the court only to astound the king by providing expensive stone for twenty altars in the Great Aten Temple. Since Akhenaten had ordained that there be countless offering tables in the open-air courts of his Aten temple, he was mightily pleased. Dozens of courtiers followed Pendua's example, but Pendua had been the first and reaped the benefit of his creative strategy. He became overseer of the cattle of the Aten, and scribe of the king, two lucrative posts. Another appointment made him administrator of the vineyards of the great royal wife.

Kysen sighed and rubbed his forehead. He twisted around, lay on his stomach, and grabbed a stack of letters from the queen's correspondence during her last year. These were among the few that hadn't been left behind when the court abandoned Horizon of the Aten. One of them mentioned Prince Usermontu, another parvenu who had attracted Meren's suspicion.

As a youth Usermontu had been known to make fun of Akhenaten's clumsiness, his horselike face and sagging stomach. Once Akhenaten became heir and later king, Usermontu had found himself outside the intimate circle of royal friends. Then one morning early in Akhenaten's reign Usermontu had experienced a mystic revelation. During worship at the new sun temple the king had caused to be constructed on the doorstep of the temple of Amun, Usermontu had been seized by a vision. He staggered to pharaoh and fell at his feet, reciting Aten prayers and shivering at the same time. Regurgitating the litany written by Akhenaten, the prince had claimed that the power of pharaoh had possessed him.

Meren told Kysen the story with the comment that it was lucky for Usermontu that he'd claimed possession by the king's power rather than the Aten's. The king reserved to himself all communion with the sun disk, but few had grasped the significance of this nuance at first. Meren had admired Usermontu's creativity, but he deplored the way the prince had turned on the old gods and helped Akhenaten disestablish the temples and impoverish the priests.

Prince Usermontu gained the title of Friend of the King as well as the stewardship of several royal estates. Shortly before the queen's death Usermontu had been given the responsibility of the queen's horses and for appointing and managing Nefertiti's bodyguards. Both he and Lord Pendua had survived Akhenaten, but they'd lost their posts in the transition under Tutankhamun. They attended court and constantly sought positions and favor from pharaoh, but each had been too enthusiastic in his quest for riches at the expense of the old gods. Tutankhamun granted them small benefits, but his ministers advised against elevating either Prince Usermontu or Lord Pendua. One of those giving the advice was Meren. Kysen set aside Meren's notes and reached for an old report on the lesser servants of the queen.

"You've been in here for hours. What are you doing on the floor?"

Kysen sat up to find his sister Bener coming toward him. She was dressed for work in a plain shift, and a simple faience necklace was her only ornament. She was tall for a girl, almost as tall as Kysen. Meren said she resembled her mother with her quick movements and commanding manner. Bener had a habit of twirling her hair around her finger when she was agitated, but her most annoying habit was interfering in the affairs of her father when she should be concerned with running the house. Kysen frowned at her as she plopped down beside him and began inspecting Meren's notes.

"You interrupted me," he said.

"You weren't doing anything."

Kysen's frown turned to a scowl. "I was thinking."

"About the queen's killer?"

"Shhh!"

"Don't hiss at me," Bener said. "We're alone and there's no chance we'll be overheard."

"Father was furious with you the last time you interfered."

"Why are you rubbing your head?"

Kysen searched his sister's face, noted the concern, and sighed again. "Reading all these records has made it ache."

"You should talk instead. Rest your eyes."

"I can't discuss this with you."

"Yes you can. I won't tell anyone. I never reveal Father's secrets."

It was true. Bener knew some of Meren's most dangerous secrets and remained silent. Kysen massaged his temples and relented.

"I've managed to lose the merchant Dilalu."

"I know."

Kysen gave her an irritated look and continued. "I've got men looking for him. Then there's Zulaya. Father sent a man to find him at his country estate, but he wasn't there. Evidently he spends little time there. His mother was Egyptian, but his father was Babylonian, and he moves about according to the demands of trade."

"Zulaya is one of the men Othrys said might be involved in the queen's death?"

"Yes," Kysen said. "He's a wealthy merchant who deals with the temples, Asiatic princes, the kings of Assyria, Babylon, and of course the Hittite king. He trades Egyptian grain, linen, and natron for timber from Byblos, copper from Cyprus, oil and wine from Syria, olive oil from the Greeks. The temple of Amun sometimes uses his services as a trader to exchange gold for unguents, resin, aromatic woods, whatever they require."

"Then he shouldn't be hard to find."

"Except that he has many agents who work for him and seldom needs to come to Memphis himself. He may be here now, but his affairs take him to the delta, to Nubia, to many places. But we'll find him, although I doubt he'll be of much help. He only began trading in Egypt about ten years ago when he purchased an estate here."

"And before that?"

"I don't know. It's not important, Bener. He must have made his fortune among the Asiatics and decided to try his luck among his mother's people. Othrys seems to think Zulaya is dangerous, a dealer in secret power, and capable of causing us the kind of trouble we've been having since we began to search for this evil one."

Bener set aside the documents she'd been reviewing. "Othrys doesn't spend his time at court. That's where you should look for the person who ordered her death."

"Obviously," Kysen snapped. He hated it when Bener pointed out to him things he already knew. "But until we told pharaoh what we were doing, questioning great men wasn't possible. Even Father can't haul Prince Usermontu into this office and demand an accounting of his time during Nefertiti's illness without pharaoh's permission."

"And now?"

"And now Father will do that once he returns from Syene. I can't do it."

"Of course not."

They lapsed into silence.

Bener picked up a rush pen that Kysen had set on the scribe's palette he'd been using. "Usermontu and Lord Pendua. Hmm." She pointed the pen at Meren's notes. "What about these other names."

"Lady Takemet was known to have been jealous of Nefertiti's power and beauty, but she's dead."

"Princess Sitamun?" Bener gave him a look of astonishment.

Kysen nodded. "I know. What are we going to do? She's the daughter of Amunhotep the Magnificent and Queen

Tiye, the sister of the pharaoh. Father says she blamed Nefertiti for failing to stop Akhenaten's excesses."

"But she's a royal princess!"

"You think princesses aren't capable of having someone killed?"

"But why?" Bener protested. "She would gain nothing from Nefertiti's death."

"Nothing we can discern at the moment," Kysen said. "But Father thinks it's more likely to be someone else. Nefertiti's chief Aten priest, Thanuro, for example. Evidently he was a serpent, always spying on her, one of the fanatics who excelled at looting the old temples. But he retired not long before Akhenaten died. And he's dead too."

Bener picked up Meren's notes again. "It says here that Father tried to trace him. Ten years ago when he retired he received a gift from pharaoh, an estate near Byblos, and he died on his way to take possession of it. That was the year after the queen was murdered. Imagine dying away from Egypt in some Canaanite wasteland where there are no embalmer priests."

"All we know is that a scribe from the garrison at Byblos wrote to announce his death from an ague. He joined a caravan heading in the direction of his new estate, but the caravan was attacked and returned to Byblos. I suppose he was entombed there."

"What of these?" Bener asked, pointing to a list of names.

"Two were in Nubia during the relevant time, one is dead. I'm more concerned with Prince Usermontu. He was a captain of troops and overseer of the horses of the queen. The queen disliked him because he beat his wife. She ordered him to cease, and when he didn't she arranged for the poor woman to obtain a divorce. Nefertiti ordered Usermontu to pay one third of his estate to his wife, and he never forgot it. He greatly enriched himself under Akhenaten. Father thinks he must have gained half a dozen new estates."

Bener raised her eyebrows. "A man with much to lose."

"Indeed."

"So," Bener said, "these are the men still alive who were present in Horizon of the Aten and who had a reason to kill the queen—Dilalu, Pendua, and Usermontu. What of Zulaya?"

Kysen shrugged. "Father is interested in him because Othrys suggested he had the power to cause the kind of trouble we've been having. But if he's involved, it must be indirectly, since he had no contact with the queen."

"Perhaps I can find out more," Bener said. She set the papyri aside and rose. "Dilalu and Zulaya may be secretive, but they're rich men. They employ servants, and servants talk, and it will be easy to find out about Prince Usermontu and Lord Pendua."

Kysen jumped to his feet and shook a finger at her. "No. I forbid it."

Bener merely raised an eyebrow.

"Father has forbidden you to interfere! If you get yourself in trouble he'll blame me."

"I'll tell him it wasn't your fault, but I'm not going to get into trouble."

Groaning, Kysen said, "I'll have you followed."

"Oh, very well. If you must be difficult about this, I'll come to you with anything I devise, and you can carry out my plan."

Kysen bit his lip, pondering the likelihood of any of Bener's schemes being any good. He smiled. "We have an agreement."

"Excellent, then you'd better be on your way."

"On my way? Where?"

Bener paused as she opened the office door. "Oh, did I forget to tell you? The king sent word that he wishes to bestow a gift upon Father for saving his life. You're to go to the workshop of the royal jeweler Basa."

"Damnation, Bener, why didn't you tell me sooner?"

"You have time," she replied calmly. "It's hours before sunset."

Grumbling under his breath, Kysen left word of his destination with a charioteer and set out for the jeweler's. Basa, like many of the finest master craftsmen, had been well rewarded for his talents. He lived near the temple of Ptah in a large house that also contained his workshop. Kysen took the long avenue that led to the temple, skirted the boundary wall, and hurried down the Street of the Twin Moons. Giving his name to the porter at the gate, he was led down a short path, past a shrine to Ptah, and into the house itself. The anteroom was crowded with customers, each being attended to by an assistant. Above their conversation Kysen could hear the pounding of dozens of hammers, the grating of saws, and the whoosh of bellows coming from the workshops behind the house.

A porter immediately led Kysen into the reception hall and to the lustration area where he could wash away the grime of the streets. Two men conferred over a papyrus on a table beside the master's dais. When he was ready, the porter preceded him to the table.

As he approached, the men turned. One was the master jeweler, Basa. The other was an Asiatic dressed in a long robe that stretched from his neck to his ankles. Diagonal folds of the finest blue wool hugged his body, and appliqués in geometric forms glittered from the fabric. A headband of the same design bound his long hair. He wore a beard arranged in a profusion of tight coils that concealed his face from nose to chin, except for dark lips that had pressed together as Kysen approached. His feet were encased in gilded sandals, and thick electrum bands encircled his ankles.

The jeweler bowed to him. "Ah, great one, you honor my poor house. May the blessings of Amun shower you."

"Greetings, Basa."

"Lord Kysen, this is Zulaya, who has presented me with a commission from the temple of Amun."

Taken unaware, Kysen managed to conceal his surprise at this unexpected encounter. Zulaya's reaction was hidden, for he'd swept down into a bow the moment the jeweler began speaking. He straightened to reveal an expression with all the impassivity of a lizard. Kysen studied him closely. Zulaya exuded the confidence one might expect from a wealthy man, but there was something more. Kysen sensed power, watchfulness, and a burning intensity. Most, however, would detect only the man's air of cosmopolitan polish, and Kysen almost began to feel he was imagining Zulaya's controlled wariness.

Basa was rattling on. "Zulaya trades throughout the world and brings rare treasures to Egypt, Lord Kysen. Should you require timber or fine wines, anything, he can provide it."

Zulaya bowed again. "You flatter me, Basa. I'm sure the son of the Eyes and Ears of Pharaoh has his own traders. May I inquire after the health of the great Lord Meren?"

"He has been ill, but he's recovering," Kysen said.

"One of my ships has brought health-enhancing herbs from Cyprus. I will send some."

"My thanks, Zulaya, but Lord Meren is away from Memphis at the moment."

Zulaya inclined his head. "They will be sent so that his physician may use them upon his return."

The garrulous Basa interrupted. "Zulaya plies his trade

all over the Great Green. I swear he must have a hundred ships."

"You exaggerate," Zulaya said smoothly. "I have a few poor vessels, and they pale beside the great Byblos ships of pharaoh."

Kysen was thinking quickly. He should express interest in some commodity and have Zulaya come to Golden House for an exchange agreement. It would be the perfect excuse to find out more about him, especially since Meren was away. Not long ago Zulaya had accidentally met Meren at the Divine Lotus. His father had been in disguise; he'd been accused of trying to kill pharaoh. But Zulaya shouldn't be allowed to see him and connect Lord Meren with the man from the tavern. There was no way to predict what the merchant might make of the famous Lord Meren haunting the disreputable tavern in the guise of a Greek pirate.

"Zulaya, I do have a request," he said, as if suddenly remembering. "My sister Tefnut, who will give birth shortly, requires fine cedar for new chairs and tables. Also, I would like to purchase oil and wine for my father's stores in his houses at Thebes, Memphis, and in the delta. This is an urgent requirement. Perhaps I could see you tomorrow."

"Unfortunately—"

"Don't be hasty," Basa said. "I know you were to deliver that lapis lazuli to me, but I can wait one more day. It would be my honor to be of service to Lord Meren."

Something flickered behind Zulaya's eyes. There was a slight pause, almost imperceptible, and then the merchant bowed again.

"Ishtar has smiled upon me this day," he said. "I will present myself at Golden House tomorrow, Lord Kysen."

Kysen gave him a smile as smooth and seamless as a block

of granite from the quarries at Syene. "Better still, I can receive you now, as soon as I am finished here."

"Ah, but fate does not smile upon hasty arrangements,
Lord Kysen."

It took all his will to remember he wasn't a common son
of a tomb worker. He met Zulaya's intense gaze with one
that assumed a natural right to command. "I won't be long.
You may wait for me in the reception room."

Zulaya's gaze flattened. He bowed his head. "As the lord
commands."

With a quick nod to Basa, Zulaya backed away from
Kysen, turned, and walked swiftly out of the room. As he
began to discuss the king's gift with Basa, Kysen wondered
if he'd made a dangerous mistake.

Chapter 7

Meren lay on his back across the mats that had served as the table for their midday meal, and as their bed. His forearm shielded his eyes, and he listened to the noise Anath was making in her search of one last room. Every muscle ached with that special weariness peculiar to intimate release, and for once the clamor of thoughts in his heart had quieted.

Anath had given him this gift. Unlike Bentanta, who treated him like a youth in need of lessons in manners, Anath asked him for his strength and gave hers in return. She gave without demanding answers or promises or trying to force him to reveal more than he wished. Easy, light of heart, she had come to him, shared herself, and let him go, gently, but with the understanding that neither of them required feverish revelations or expressions of romantic attachment.

Since his wife died he'd been with many women. Most of them had been ladies who expressed interest and had no other attachment; he never dallied with innocents. Some-

times one of the household maids would try to catch his
attention, but he'd learned long ago that such encounters encouraged the recipient to make unsuitable demands and
caused jealousy in the household. Jealousy interfered with
the smooth running of Golden House and risked disrup-
tion of routine or worse.

Anath was different. She came to him freely and with no
other thought than pleasure and solace. She had confided
in him her weariness of living abroad, but the next moment
she regaled him with tales of grasping Babylonian merchants
and the ridiculous rivalries of petty princes. Then she admitted that if she came home she would miss watching the
continuous folly of the Asiatics.

Meren remembered her description of Burnaburiash, the
king of Babylon. His majesty was aging and hated the idea
so much that he tinted his hair to cover the gray. He also
refused to admit he wasn't as agile as he'd once been. Rather
than refrain from activities beyond his endurance he insisted
upon sword practice and exercise with the army. Inevitably
he pulled a muscle or strained his back and had to be carried back to his palace where he lay moaning and complaining for weeks. Instead of learning from this experience,
once he recovered he would trot right back out to the practice fields where he would fall over his own sword or break
the axle of his chariot. Anath said that if Burnaburiash
weren't so adept at turning his enemies against each other,
he'd have been deposed years ago. What had impressed Meren
most about her tale was that Anath, so experienced in intrigue and deception as the Eyes of Babylon, retained a light-
ness of spirit that charmed everyone who came near her.

When he listened to Anath's stories Meren had less time
to dwell upon the dark thoughts that seemed to consume
him so often. He was still smiling at the memory of Burnaburi-

ash when something heavy landed on his stomach. He grunted and lowered his arm to stare into the scarred and furry face of Khufu. Meren growled at the cat, but Khufu merely twitched an ear and settled down for a wash.

"Get off me, you foul creature," Meren muttered as he shoved the cat away.

"Are you still lying down?" Anath came in dusting her hands. "I've searched the last room and found nothing of interest. It's time to go."

"I was just coming for you," Meren said with a last glare at Khufu.

Anath came over to lean against him and slap his flat stomach. "Be kind to poor Khufu. He likes you."

"That animal likes no one but you. It's obvious from his appearance that he lives to do battle." Khufu stuck his misshapen nose in the air and stalked out of the room.

Arguing lightly, Meren and Anath went outside to the dilapidated shelter under which they'd tethered the horses. The animals had been fed and watered, and Meren walked around the chariot and stepped into the vehicle. As he moved, a paw shot out across the floorboards. Meren's foot caught it, and he stumbled, nearly falling on his face. Dust and grit flew in at him as Khufu scrambled away to sit innocently in the shade, purring, while Meren cursed and untangled himself. A musical tumble of laughter let him know that Anath had seen the whole incident.

"It's not amusing," he snapped as he got to his feet.

Anath jumped into the chariot beside him. "Yes it is, when you consider how graceful and stately the great Lord Meren is. To see him fall on his face is a great amusement."

"One day that cat will come to an evil end," Meren muttered, but he refrained from further comment because Anath was still laughing at him.

By the time they'd left the palace battlements Meren was laughing as well. They drove back along the Royal Road and past the small North Palace, the jewel-like retreat in which Nefertiti had died. For a long time Meren's memories of Horizon of the Aten hadn't been clear. He'd deliberately shrouded them in a haze as thick as the one that hung over the eastern horizon and turned the dying solar orb into a diffuse lake of carnelian flame. It had taken many weeks of effort, much reading over records and discussion with those who had been present to restore his memory. At last he thought he had an accurate picture of the queen's final days. He hadn't realized he'd stopped the chariot until Anath spoke.

"She died there."

"Yes, she did."

Anath turned to him, her tilted eyes full of concern. "You know what happened?"

"I think so," Meren said, his mind drawn back to a day eleven years earlier.

The reception of the viceroy of Kush rivaled any of the great court ceremonies at Horizon of the Aten. In the Riverside Palace a gathering of courtiers awaited the great royal wife, Meren and Ay among them. There was to be a grand procession like that held at Akhenaten's jubilee, with Nubians bearing tribute—gold, ivory, incense, slaves, cattle, and exotic animals. Meren could hear the distant roar of lions and trumpet of elephants.

Everyone wore elaborate court dress—razor-pleated, transparent linen overrobes, heavy gold broad collars weighed down by turquoise, malachite, and lapis lazuli; long, intricately plaited wigs surmounted by diadems of electrum, gold, and silver; ceremonial daggers, scimitars, and staffs of office. The air blossomed with scents like balanos oil mixed with myrrh and resin, cardamom, sweet rush, honey, and galbanum. And hushed voices floating on the heavy scents, exchanging whispers and veiled mean-ings.

Meren waited beside his mentor, his shoulders aching with the added burden of gold draped on them. Lost in reflection, he was missing his wife Sit-Hathor and his daughters. The loneliness followed him like his shadow soul. Then trumpets blared, send-ing everyone to their knees. Meren lifted his gaze from the floor tiles when the doors from the royal suite swung open to reveal the queen. No, pharaoh.

He blinked rapidly at the strange sight. Nefertiti, now King Neferneferuaten, stood in the doorway in regal isolation. The double crown rested like a heavy tower on her head, and her hair had been gathered close so that the base of the lowest crown concealed it. She wore a false beard of gold strapped to her frag-ile chin and carried the crook and flail scepters. The sight of a woman in those crowns and that golden beard, their first since Akhenaten declared her king, caused something never heard at the appearance of an Egyptian monarch—grumbling. It began in the silence of their obeisance and grew as Nefertiti remained framed by the high vault of the doors.

Meren had lowered his gaze, but at the quiet, rolling thun-der of the courtiers he looked up at the great royal wife. Nefer-titi still hadn't moved. Her gaunt features seemed plastered like the mask of an embalmed one, pale and painted. Then Meren saw a bright flush suffuse her skin, and she licked her lips. Nef-ertiti whispered something, and a waiting woman handed her a golden cup. The queen-king drained it, but as she handed it back to her lady she sagged and placed her hand over her eyes.

The grumbling tone of the courtiers changed, shifted to cu-riosity, and several of them conferred among themselves. But no one approached Nefertiti. Meren glanced at Ay, whose gaze was fixed on his daughter. When she began to gasp for breath, he sprang out of his stillness with Meren at his side. They reached her in time to catch her as she swayed. She cried out, flailing as if blind, and fell with Ay supporting her full weight. The crowns fell from her head, and would have touched the floor had Meren not caught them. He lunged forward, grabbed them, and ended up on his knees.

A great furor exploded around him. Ay vanished with his daughter, and the nobles dispersed in panic, leaving Meren in an empty space for a moment. Then someone grabbed his arm and hauled him upright. Dazed at the experience of touching the sacred crowns of Egypt, Meren clutched them to his body and faced Thanuro, the Aten priest of Nefertiti. He deftly relieved Meren of his burden.

"Swift thinking, Lord Meren. Pharaoh will be pleased."

"She's ill," Meren blurted out.

"I didn't mean the great royal wife," Thanuro said with oiled smoothness. "His majesty, living in truth, the sole one, Akhenaten. He will be pleased."

"Yes, of course."

Without another word Thanuro glided over to the two cowering priests who held the gold boxes in which the crowns were kept. He placed each in its container, motioned to the priest, and sailed quickly out of the hall with his assistants and their royal burdens. And as he left he passed Prince Usermontu standing by an archway, leaning against the threshold, surveying the confusion with a slight smile.

Meren shook his head at the vision still clinging to his heart, of Thanuro, of Usermontu. That Thanuro had been unaffected by Nefertiti's collapse was understandable; he was Akhenaten's man. Usermontu had held a high position in the queen's household, and he'd smiled. How undiplomatic.

"Usermontu again," Anath said. "He was there when she

collapsed? He could have used the steward to get rid of Nefertiti. I told you it was worth coming here."

"Perhaps. But knowing Usermontu might have wanted the queen dead, knowing that he had the opportunity to cause her death, these things aren't enough."

"But you just said Usermontu was there," Anath protested.

"So was Lord Pendua. Dilalu was somewhere nearby. He had reason to fear Nefertiti as well. And there's Thanuro. He was in a position to carry out this plot, although I can't think why he'd do it."

"But of all whom you suspect, Usermontu is the most vicious, and he knew Nefertiti would prevent him from rising any higher in the king's favor." Khufu snaked himself around Anath's ankles, and she bent to stroke his head. She continued. "Everyone thought she had the plague, even the queen herself. You say that after a few days she insisted upon being moved here, away from pharaoh and the children. The steward and the cook came with her. So did Usermontu. Five days after that she was dead."

Meren smiled bitterly. "They were careful not to hurry her death. Ay stayed by her side until the end, and I brought messages back and forth from the king. Akhenaten wanted to be here, but the ministers protested that he would expose himself to the plague demons that haunted Nefertiti."

Anath nodded, and they both studied the facade of the North Palace. Behind the high pylon gates lay a small palace with a sunken garden. Cool, green, and intimate, it had been a place of refuge for Nefertiti. Meren hoped that the surroundings had been a comfort to her as she struggled for life.

"We must go," Meren said. He guided the chariot south, toward the central city.

In a short time they rode alongside the pylon gates of

the Great Aten Temple. The vast carvings on the ramparts depicted Akhenaten and Nefertiti worshipping the sun disk. Meren kept his gaze fixed on the road rather than look at the gigantic figure of the king with its elongated facial features, hollow shoulders, and slanting eyes. The exaggeration upon which Akhenaten had insisted mocked the harmony that art should bring to existence.

Whenever Meren gazed upon Akhenaten's reliefs he experienced the same unsettled foreboding. It was as if the chaos Akhenaten brought to Egypt took form in his art and spread distortion, perversion, and imbalance. Worst of all was looking at the king's eyes. Against the pure white background paint those slanting eyes absorbed light and produced a gleaming darkness, chaos, and madness. It didn't help that the eye on the pylon gate was as large as Meren's head.

He was glad when they left the temple behind and passed under the Royal Bridge. Meren guided the chariot around the Great Palace complex and down to the docks where Kenro, Dedi, and Bek waited for them. Each bore a box or document case, indicating that their search had yielded more than Anath and Meren's. After everyone boarded *Wings of Horus*, Meren held a meeting under the deckhouse awning.

Kenro spoke for the scribes. "We gathered everything that might have significance, lord, but we're not finished."

"We should stay until the task is complete," Anath said. She was lying on a couch beneath the awning while a sailor fanned her.

"Kenro and the others will stay here to continue the work," Meren replied. "I must go to Syene. An old friend is expecting me. Go on, Kenro."

The scribe held up two halves of a torn papyrus scroll. "This is from the King's House magazines. It's a list of ration increases during the period before and just after the queen died. The lord will see why we kept it." He handed it to Meren.

Meren read down the list of dates, names, and amounts of grain, olive oil, lamp oil, natron, and other commodities. He found the names and titles of Prince Usermontu and Thanuro. Usermontu's rations had been increased by half shortly after Nefertiti died; Thanuro's had been doubled. Lord Pendua had received the right to a daily allowance of lamp oil from the Aten temple, a lucrative grant.

Akhenaten had dispensed largesse to his minions far more frequently than other pharaohs. Meren had always suspected it was the king's way of keeping his followers dependent and loyal. If one did away with the sacred underpinnings of kingship, one must replace them with something. Riches seemed a practical alternative. Meren glanced at the other amounts on the scroll. The increases given to the suspects were much larger than those given to most of the king's servants.

Kenro produced a clay tablet covered with the wedge-shaped script of the Asiatics. "This is a letter from the king of Assyria promising to send a pair of thoroughbreds to Prince Usermontu."

"Usermontu was a friend of the king of Assyria?" Anath asked.

"No," Meren said. "Lesser kings often send gifts to men they think might influence pharaoh."

"There are more tablets, lord, but I haven't had time to translate them," Kenro said. "I did find one from the prince of Byblos promising to extend his hospitality to pharaoh's retiring servant, Thanuro."

"Hardly of interest," Anath said with a yawn. "I'm going back to my ship to wash off this road dust."

Bek handed Kenro several sheets of torn papyrus.

"Oh, and we did find these." Kenro leafed through the sheets. "A report on the audit of the queen's household after her death, conducted by the steward Wah, a transfer of that Asiatic estate to the priest in year sixteen, a letter from the queen to the prince of Byblos regarding a missing shipment of gold she sent to him."

With another yawn Anath held out her hand to Meren. "Excellent work. Your servants are to be commended, Lord Meren, but I fear I grow weary and must rest."

Meren conducted Anath off the ship and returned to his scribes. "So, we know Thanuro was well-rewarded for his service to pharaoh. Too bad he died. He would have been an excellent witness, and it doesn't seem we're going to find anything useful among all this litter."

"Perhaps there's information in some of the records we haven't examined, lord." Kenro indicated the boxes and document cases lying on the deck.

"Keep looking. I'm sailing in the morning, and I'll come back for you on my way back to Memphis."

"Yes, lord."

Meren dismissed the scribes and retired to the deckhouse. It had been fitted with embroidered wall hangings, colorful woven mats, and a folding camp bed. A feather-stuffed mattress rested on the bed with soft linen sheets covering it. Meren's body servant, Zar, was waiting for him with cool water and washing cloths. Meren bathed and dressed in a fresh kilt before going outside to compose letters to pharaoh and Kysen. Each was a report on his progress, not that there was much of it. Meren regretted allowing Anath to convince him to make this side trip. His presence hadn't been necessary.

But then you wouldn't have been with her at the Riverside Palace.

Meren felt his lips stretch into a smile. *Stop that. Your men will catch you wearing the grin of a fool and know everything.* Clearing his throat, Meren dipped his rush pen in the black inkwell on his scribe's palette and began to write his report to pharaoh. By sunset he'd finished. He had a meal with the ship's captain, a heavy one that comprised spicy fish soup, roasted heron, salad greens in oil, fresh bread, and date cakes. They shared thick black beer flavored with dates, and when his eyelids grew heavy he retired to his bed.

He drifted off to sleep and plunged into an erotic dream in which Anath straddled him, her uptilted eyes laughing. Groaning, Meren tried to turn over, but a great weight pinned him. His eyes flew open, and he stared up at the laughing eyes from his dream.

"The Eyes of Pharaoh shouldn't sleep," Anath said as she straddled his hips. She shrugged out of a transparent shift, bent over him, and snaked her tongue into his mouth. "Terrible demons lurk in the shadows waiting to pounce."

Meren allowed her to kiss him, but pulled free to say, "It's late, and we have to sail in the morning."

"Unless you're going to row this ship with the sailors, I don't see a difficulty," Anath replied.

When Meren opened his mouth to argue she covered it with her fingers. "No one refuses the Eyes of Babylon."

Meren gasped as she touched him.

"Certainly not me," he said, and he stopped arguing.

Chapter 8

Kysen lounged on the roof of Golden House, his expression carefully pleasant, his attitude one of amused attention as Bener told Zulaya tales about her sisters and Kysen's son, Remi. Beneath his calm facade he was furious and couldn't wait to flay Bener with his tongue the moment they were alone. He hadn't intended to make this man a familiar, but Bener hadn't consulted him. She'd welcomed their unexpected guest as if he were a personal friend when Kysen had brought him home. Then she'd launched into an imitation of a grand lady, mistress of a noble house, and invited Zulaya to the evening meal.

Having discussed Kysen's purchases, Zulaya had been persuaded to spend time in Meren's private garden, one of the most luxurious in the Two Lands. Kysen conducted his guest down the avenue of pomegranate trees that led to the refuge, all the while keeping their conversation innocuous. They discussed the cost of ebony and the amount of time it would take to receive a shipment of cedar from Byblos. When the tour of the garden led them to the arbor covered with grapevines Zulaya talked about the merits of Syrian wine.

"Your travels take you across vast distances," Kysen said, hoping to begin his questioning without being detected. "Such interminable journeying must become wearisome. I hope you're comfortable in Memphis."

"Indeed, most honored lord," Zulaya said as he touched a grape leaf.

Having failed to elicit where the man was staying in the city, Kysen tried again. "Is there one place in which you remain for long? To rest, that is?"

"I am fortunate to have a house in Byblos," Zulaya said.

"But you're half Egyptian, I hear."

Zulaya turned to smile at him. "Yes, lord. My mother was Egyptian, but of humble stock. My father came from Babylon, a trader in wool and fine ceramic wares. He came to Egypt with a caravan one year, and returned with my mother. They built a house near the ziggurat, and prospered under the benevolence of the goddess Ishtar."

"So you spent your youth in Babylon." Kysen walked with his guest toward one of the pavilions.

"I lived there until I finished school, but then I traveled with my father." Zulaya kept pace with Kysen, and his robe whipped about his ankles as the north breeze picked up. "I confess I prefer the excitement of the journey to remaining always in one place, seeing the same sights endlessly."

He paused as they reached the pavilion and glanced around the garden with its orchard, its forest of acacias, willows, perseas, and tamarisks. "However, to remain in this place . . ." He gave Kysen a rueful glance. "I thought that the weight of years would change me, and such beauty as this is tempting, but eventually I would long for the sight of the sea you call the Great Green. I hunger to see the endless line where the water meets the azure sky."

Kysen nodded and directed his steps along the edge of the largest of the reflection pools where a talapia fish darted between the papyrus reeds. "Then I wonder that you bothered to purchase land in Egypt."

"A desire to own a small portion of my mother's birth land," Zulaya said. "It's a small estate near the town of Hebenu."

"Ah, not far from Horizon of the Aten."

Zulaya wrinkled his forehead. "Yes," he said slowly, "but there is little to be said for it now that pharaoh lives here."

"My father said it was glorious in the days of the heretic."

"It must have been," the merchant said in an offhand manner.

Kysen stopped and met Zulaya's passive gaze. "I would have thought you'd seen it often, since so much trade shifted there after the city was established."

"Those were days of great unrest among the kingdoms in Syria and Canaan. My caravans met raiders at every mountain pass, and I was preoccupied with the task of protecting them. I never went farther than the delta after year four of that reign." Zulaya gave him a wry look. "I almost lost my fortune at least three times, to bandits under the protection of worthless city chiefs."

"But the gods protected you," Kysen said as he headed out of the garden.

"I sacrificed to them many times a day for several years."

After they returned to the house, servants swept Zulaya away to be bathed and perfumed. By the time the sun set Bener had taken charge of them and led the way to the roof where the smell of roasting meat greeted them. By now Kysen had been in Zulaya's company for several hours, during which he'd assessed the man.

The merchant was a strange mixture of foreign and familiar. He dressed expensively and wore jewels of Asiatic and Egyptian origin. Gold bracelets encircled his arms, each engraved with Babylonian motifs—rosettes, bees, and dogs, the symbol of the goddess Gula. Yet from Zulaya's neck hung an Egyptian pectoral necklace bearing the symbol of the moon, a hollow rectangle of gold beads into which had been mounted an electrum moon disk floating on the crescent new moon.

The mixture of Egyptian and Asiatic went deeper than ornamentation, however. Zulaya had the long, narrow head of an Egyptian, as well as a slight stature, but his hair curled in ringlets rather than waves, a more Asiatic trait. Kysen hadn't noticed his accent when they first met, but now he could detect it by the slightly more guttural sound to his speech. Beyond the physical, Kysen had marked Zulaya's assured manner. Kysen had puzzled over this easy demeanor since meeting the man, until he realized that Zulaya moved among the trappings of nobility as if he belonged there. He didn't gawk at Meren's ebony and gold furnishings, at the luxurious garden filled with priceless myrrh and frankincense shrubs, at the house that was nearly as large as a palace.

As Kysen observed his guest with Bener he realized the man was older than he'd first seemed. His hair was sprinkled with silver. Delicate lines spread like solar rays from the corners of his eyes. He sprinkled his conversation with humor in a manner that made him seem younger. He certainly had no trouble entertaining Bener. She had drawn her chair closer to her guest, and her gaze seldom left him as Zulaya related some tale of a pirate raid on one of his ships.

"We shot flaming arrows onto the deck as they tried to come alongside. That usually fends them off, unless they risk firing them first."

Bener was wide-eyed. "Do they?"

"Sometimes." Zulaya leaned toward her, his eyes crinkling with amusement. "It isn't wise to set fire to the ship that carries the very thing you wish to steal, but some pirates have the wits of oxen." He popped a grape in his mouth. "Whichever ship survives the fire is the ship I take into port."

"Amazing," Bener said with a rapid flutter of her dark lashes.

Kysen eyed her as Zulaya bowed to her from his chair. After a quiet moment he suddenly asked, "And the pirates?"

Zulaya waved his wine cup. "Most of them are killed."

"No prisoners?"

"Oh, a few," Zulaya said lightly. "When I began to have trouble with them I devised a method for dealing with them. Those who attacked and lived I divided into three groups. The first I flayed alive while the others watched; the second I hung from the bow of my ship by their feet as an example to all who saw them; and the others I released to spread stories of the fate of their companions."

Bener swallowed hard and turned to pick among the dessert cakes on a tray.

Kysen merely nodded. "Effective."

"Not as effective as my other method." Zulaya grinned at him. "I found a pirate named Othrys and paid him to keep the others away. Perhaps you've heard of him?"

Meeting Zulaya's gaze with an open and blank look, Kysen shook his head. "No, but there are so many lawless men at sea."

"True."

The night was growing cooler, and from the roof flickering points of lamplight sprinkled the city. Near the river, torches sent rippling sprays of gold across the water.

Zulaya gazed out at the city and sighed. "I regret I must take my leave. I have promised to attend the high priest of Ptah early tomorrow."

The merchant thanked Bener for her hospitality, and Kysen walked downstairs with him.

"I regret not having the honor of being presented to Lord Meren," Zulaya said as they walked across the reception hall. He stopped and turned to Kysen as they neared the master's dais with its costly chair of cedar, ebony, ivory, and gold. "I confess to a great admiration of your father, Lord Kysen."

Kysen was taken aback. "Oh?"

"Indeed. Lord Meren's skills are celebrated throughout the empire and in every land, of course, but I particularly appreciate your father's fine grasp of the intricacies of the power struggles among great men. We humble merchants are greatly affected by quarrels and strife among the mighty, you know."

"I had no idea that foreign merchants took such an interest in Lord Meren."

Zulaya inclined his head. "Among my people it is rare to come upon a nobleman whose loyalty to his prince isn't motivated by greed—for riches or power. Your father's character is well known, Lord Kysen. Of him it is said that he cares for the pharaoh of Egypt out of reverence, never seeking the Gold of Honor or other rewards. Everyone knows that Lord Meren honors justice and order, and allows neither high place nor sentiment to sway him from his principles."

"Yes," Kysen said. He led the merchant to the front door.

"My father is a man of great honor, but I'm surprised that his reputation has spread as far as you say."

"When so rare a man is found, word of his existence travels far."

With a low bow, Zulaya was gone. As the porter shut the door Kysen shook his head. He didn't think Zulaya was the kind of man to try to squirm into his favor with flattery. The man had meant what he said, which was surprising, given Zulaya's ruthlessness and proven ability to amass a fortune by less than honest means. His association with pirates like Othrys wasn't simply one of convenience. Zulaya bought looted goods from them and passed them off as legitimate. Perhaps the merchant's admiration was that of a powerful man who respected the strength of another.

Kysen headed for the roof again, deep in thought. Zulaya was formidable. He'd just spent hours in Golden House without revealing anything of importance, despite Kysen's probing questions. Without flattering himself, Kysen could claim great skill at eliciting information from suspects, yet the most to which Zulaya would admit was consorting with pirates. Such verbal fencing was worthy of a royal emissary, of Meren himself. Indeed, Zulaya and his father had much in common—skill at intrigue, charm, ruthlessness.

Kysen reached the roof intent on taking Bener to task for her interference with Zulaya, only to find the eating tables deserted except for the serving maids. He searched for her, but she'd gone to her chamber. Before he could hunt her down, his son appeared with his nurse. Kysen spent the rest of the evening with the boy. By this time it was too late to fight with his sister, so he went to bed feeling cheated of his opportunity to tell Bener what he thought of her.

His sore head kept him awake so that he slept late the next day. It was mid-morning by the time he had break-

fasted, and there was still not word on Dilalu. He wanted
to talk to Bener, but she had gone out. He spent the rest
of the morning conducting the business of the Eyes and
Ears of Pharaoh, all the while fuming at the delay in taking his sister to task. He wanted to see her before he set
out to find the pirate Othrys. When she finally came home
with several servants trailing behind her carrying goods from
the market, Kysen met her in the reception hall.

"Where have you been?" he snapped.

Bener raised her eyebrows, and Kysen bit off his next
comment. She dismissed her servants and poured herself a
cup of water from a jar draped with a lotus garland.

Kysen waited for the servants to leave before speaking
again. "Where have you been?"

"To the market, obviously." Bener took a long sip of water
and sighed as she sat down on the edge of the master's dais.

"I want to talk to you about last night."

"Aren't you interested in where else I've been?"

"No," Kysen said.

"You should be."

Kysen narrowed his eyes. "Why?"

"Because I've been visiting Lady Wenher."

"Pendua's wife! Curse you, Bener. You can't do that."

"Nonsense," Bener replied as she wiped perspiration from
her brow and chin. "I can, and I did. Wenher has a great
store of herbs and is well versed in their use in cooking and
medicines. Everybody knows that. Did you ever think of that
when you considered whether Lord Pendua might have—"

"Shh!" Kysen glanced around the hall, then motioned for
Bener to follow him. He led the way to Meren's office, past
the charioteer on guard there, and shut the door. "Now,
what were you saying about Lady Wenher?"

Bener shrugged. "Just that she knows a lot about herbs,

including the tekau plant you said was used to poison . . ." Bener lowered her voice. ". . . to poison the queen."

Kysen rolled his eyes, speechless.

"You asked her about the tekau plant?" he said with a groan.

"No, you fool. I asked her for a remedy for your aching head. I told her you were injured practicing close combat with the charioteers, and she had lots of advice." Bener's eyes lit. "You mix frankincense, cumin, fresh bread, goose fat, honey, and sweet beer, strain it and drink it for four days."

"Bener."

"You can also make an unguent of cumin with moringa oil, myrrh, lotus flowers, juniper berries, and—"

"Bener!"

She grinned at him. "There was tekau hanging in the room Wenher uses to dry her herbs."

Uttering a wordless sound of frustration, Kysen made no objection when his sister sauntered out of the room. Just then a document case full of royal dispatches arrived, but he was still fuming an hour later when he heard noise coming from the roof. It sounded like Bener, so he climbed the stairs to investigate.

When he got to the roof he followed the sound of her raised voice and found her hanging over the roof ledge waving and laughing. Kysen slowed as he drew near, for Bener was wearing her best robes and jewelry. She'd painted her eyes, reddened her cheeks and lips, and wore her most elaborate wig. As he gawked at her Bener gave a rippling laugh and threw a lotus flower to someone below. Kysen looked down, and watched a young man in a chariot catch the lotus and bow to his sister.

On this side of the house the distance to a wide avenue wasn't great. Young noblemen used this street to parade in their chariots harnessed with their finest thoroughbred teams. Well-born young ladies strolled by admiring the men, flirting and giggling to each other. The fortunate girls who lived on the avenue could view the scene from their roofs, and be seen to great advantage. This parading and flirting had gone on for centuries, and was one of the ways in which young Egyptians searched for potential mates. But Bener had always scoffed at the girls who simpered and giggled as they strutted on the avenue. Her most scathing remarks had targeted the girls on the roofs who hung over the ledges and flaunted themselves, and now she was making a spectacle of herself.

Bener called out a goodbye to the young man in the chariot and waved as he saluted her and drove down the avenue.

"What are you doing? Are you mad?" Kysen said as he joined her side. "First you entertain Zulaya like an old friend, then you visit Pendua's wife, and now you flirt with a stranger."

Bener hardly glanced at him. Turning on her heel, she walked away as she said, "That, dear brother, wasn't a stranger." She turned and smiled at him. "That was Lord Rudu, the eldest son of Prince Usermontu."

In a flash of gold, carnelian, and turquoise, Bener tossed Kysen a lotus flower and left him alone on the roof with the scent of frankincense and honey lingering in his nostrils.

Chapter 9

Meren woke late the morning after Anath surprised him in his bed. His late rising delayed the hour of departure, but by midday *Wings of Horus* set sail. This time Meren commanded a fast rowing pace, and the black ship cut through the north-flowing current, scattering lesser vessels before her. The journey took him down the length of Egypt, past dozens of towns and villages, until he came to Abydos, the city of Osiris. He stopped only briefly at his country estate. Then he headed south again and passed mighty Thebes, home of Amun, king of the gods. Equaled only by pharaoh's great ships, *Wings of Horus* pressed on, relentlessly breasting the force of the river, using the north breeze to push ever closer to Syene, the capital city of the first nome of Egypt.

Even though he pushed the sailors as hard as he dared, Meren didn't reach the first nome for almost two weeks. After the first night she came to his bed, he gave up trying to preserve a facade of decorum with Anath. The woman had no shyness in her, it seemed. He even grew accustomed to the amused glances of his charioteers. Once he overheard several of them.

"It should have happened long ago. Golden House needs a mistress."

"He couldn't forget his wife."

"No, it wasn't that. He had to be careful. Too many place-seekers threw their pretty daughters at him in order to make an advantageous alliance. It's the same with Lord Kysen and his daughters."

Meren had reddened upon hearing his private life discussed, even by men to whom he entrusted his life. It was a hazard of rank, this lack of privacy, and one of the reasons he refrained from too much indulgence. Circumspection and moderation protected him from scandal and left him invulnerable to coercion by anyone seeking to control the Eyes and Ears of Pharaoh. Anath ignored his remoteness as well as his dignity and severity. She simply came to him when she wanted to, regardless of what he or anyone else might think. And Meren allowed her visits.

To his surprise Anath even had the magical power to banish for a time his anxiety over the king. He spent long, tranquil days under the deckhouse awning. The jewel-blue water surrounded him; the cool wind brought air suffused with sweetness uncontaminated by the city smells of animal dung and refuse. He could lie on a couch with Anath sitting on pillows on the deck beside him while the Black Land sped by.

He watched farmers as they scurried over the fields, damming water, making ready for planting. He followed the progress of peasants on donkeys. The riders' legs hung down over the sides of their mounts, almost touching the ground. The animals plodded on the narrow paths between fields and he wondered idly where the travelers were going. He listened to the rushing sound of the water until he dozed, then woke to the sight of one of the Nile's many small islands lush with vegetation and thick with birds—crested herons, bitterns, egrets, cormorants. Anath had pointed out a black-beaked Horus falcon. Meren couldn't remember the last time he'd paid attention to birds, watched tall reeds on the shore or on the islands waving in the wind as he sailed by, or turned his face to the breeze and breathed deeply, allowing the tranquillity of the Nile to seep into his bones.

The idyll ended when the lush black fields grew scarce, the deep green of tree and water plant vanished, and the desert crept close to the shore. Eventually barren rock shoved itself right into the river, and Meren knew that Syene was near. When rounded, red granite boulders thrust themselves out of the earth, out of the Nile itself, he knew they'd arrived. At that moment he felt apprehension descend again, and he fought off images of pharaoh's features grown more haggard with each day that passed. He and Anath watched from the deck as barges carrying obelisks and colossal statues floated past them on their way south. Dark-skinned, graceful Nubians plied the waters in their smaller sailing craft and traded from their perpendicular mud houses. They had reached the gateway to the frontier of Nubia, land of gold and rebellious tribes.

From Syene, at the first Nile cataract, southward into Nubia stretched the great border fortresses, Miam, Buhen, Semna, Shaat, Tombos, all the way to Napata at the fourth cataract. From these massive bastions Egypt controlled the routes to the desert gold and copper mines, the quarries from which came precious red granite and amethyst, and managed a trade rich in exotic goods—ivory, animal skins, spices, ostrich feathers, and minerals. From nomadic traders came cattle and goats. Just as important, no one could enter

Egypt without passing the garrisons that perched on rocky promontories overlooking the narrow river valley or the troops that ceaselessly patrolled the deserts.

"There it is," Meren said, and he pointed to the island rising out of the lapis lazuli waters. "Elephantine Island."

"It doesn't look like an elephant," Anath said as she stood beside him.

"It's named for the ivory trade, foolish one."

Feeling his treasured serenity ebb from him, Meren contained his impatience while *Wings of Horus* floated slowly up to a mooring place. Elephantine was a great trading center as well as the home of a garrison in the fortress on the south end of the island high above the city. Also at the southern end of the island exquisite Egyptian temples nestled among the palm trees, one of them built by Tutankhamun's father. And not far from the fortress lay the house of the man Meren had come all this way to see—Taharqa.

Taharqa was a chief's son and the highest official in the administration of pharaoh's viceroy of Nubia, who governed the lands south of Egypt and controlled the royal gold mines. Born in far southern Nubia, which was known as Kush, he had been sent to court to be raised as an Egyptian. It was from this palace childhood that Meren knew him.

Pharaohs had long ago found that turning the children of warlike Nubian chiefs into Egyptian aristocrats assured royal control of this valuable border land. Gradually over the centuries Egyptian civilization had spread south, and now Nubian towns, temples, and fortresses looked very much like Egyptian ones. When Meren and Anath disembarked and finally reached the home of Taharqua, they saw a replica of a wealthy Egyptian nobleman's town house.

Taharqa himself came out to greet them, his blue-black

skin gleaming with oil, his proper Egyptian wig spangled with gold beads. "Many blessed greetings, Meren old friend." He bowed when Meren presented Anath. "My house is honored with your presence, Mistress Anath. Come, Meren, out of this cursed heat. I hate the heat, may Ra forgive me."

As elongated as a shadow in the dying sun, Taharqa had a languid grace and regal bearing. As he walked his numerous bracelets chimed and his overrobe swung about his legs. He ushered Meren and Anath into a reception hall the roof of which was supported by four wooden columns with lotus capitals. The ceiling had been painted like the sky with gold stars on a blue background, and the colors were so bright it was as if the sun illuminated them.

Having settled his guests in chairs, Taharqa sank onto a couch covered in cushions and draped with leopard skins. Above the couch a roof vent allowed the north breeze to flow directly onto Taharqa. When he felt the breeze he sighed as if making the trip outside had drained his strength. As soon as he lay down, servants surrounded him, plying fans, dabbing his face with a moist cloth, offering a cup of wine. Anath gave Meren a quizzical look.

"Not all Nubians are like those in the royal guard," he whispered to her.

"My head aches from the heat," Taharqa said. "Where is the herbalist with that tincture?" He fluttered his fingers at one of the servants. "Find her before I perish from the pain." Taharqa took another sip of wine and waved at the food that had been set before his guests. "Eat, drink, and refresh yourselves."

Knowing Taharqa had something he wanted to say and was approaching the subject in his usual sideways manner, Meren tore a piece of bread from a loaf and drank some of the wine that had been poured into his goblet. Anath toyed with a date, but didn't touch her cup.

Taharqa spoke of the increase in traffic from south to north since pharaoh began restoration of the temples. He asked after Meren's family and plied Anath with questions about Babylon. Then the herbalist arrived, a gray-haired Egyptian woman whose thick hands were stained and roughed from years of pounding roots, leaves, and seeds with mortar and pestle.

"There you are at last," Taharqa said. "I've nearly collapsed from the pain while you took all this time to make a simple tincture. Give it to me."

Undisturbed, the herbalist handed her master a tiny cup filled with a greenish liquid. Taharqa drank it in one gulp and sighed.

"I can feel its power already." He rubbed his temples, then waved his hand. "Go away. Having you stand there scowling at me will bring back the ache."

With a snort the herbalist took back her cup and left.

"I swear by Isis and Hathor that woman is the most disagreeable wretch I've ever employed. Do you know she had the temerity to tell me I imagine these aches in my head? I have consulted many physicians and Nubian healers who all say I am beset with evil spirits that cause my suffering. And I do suffer, in my feet, my back, my belly. Truly I am greatly afflicted, and if she weren't so talented I'd have sent the woman back to Thebes where I found her." Taharqa waggled his fingers at the servants plying fans. "Faster, curse you. Those feathers are hardly moving." Without a pause he turned and eyed Meren. "I may speak freely?"

"The Eyes of Babylon knows more secrets than both of us," Meren said.

"Does she? What I want is for you to explain yourself, Meren. I hardly hear from you in months. Then suddenly I am deluged with letters full of demands. Do I know a certain half-Nubian called Sebek, once a royal guard? Where is he? Can I find him? Can I keep him safe? Tell me why I've stirred myself and risked a terrible ague or worse."

"Now, Taharqa, you know I can't. I told you in my first letter that this is a secret matter."

"That's your answer after all my trouble?" Taharqa brought the back of his hand to his forehead and sighed. "I am unappreciated. After all those years at court when I was your confidant and friend, I am reduced to a stranger, a runner of errands. My heart is broken."

"Have another tincture. I'm sure your herbalist has one that will mend your poor heart." Meren tossed his bread back on the table.

Taharqa squinted at him over his hand. "It has something to do with the court at Horizon of the Aten." When Meren said nothing, he continued. "This Sebek was the queen's guard. Did he steal? Was he a heretic?"

Anath rose, set her wine aside, and went to Taharqa. She sat beside him and started to rub his temples with her fingertips, causing her host to moan and sink down on the couch. After a few minutes of her massage, Taharqa was nearly asleep. Meren watched quietly as Anath began to talk to his friend.

"Did you find the guard Sebek?" she asked in a gentle tone.

"Of course. He furnishes donkeys to the caravans that go to the desert gold mines and amethyst quarries."

"He is here, then."

"No, he took some animals to one of the mining camps to replace ones that died. I was waiting for him to come back when Meren sent that charioteer."

"Yes," Anath breathed as she placed her palms against Taharqa's forehead and massaged.

"I told him all he had to do was wait for the wretched man to come back from the mining camp, but he scampered off to meet Sebek on his return route. Neither of them has come back yet."

"Damnation," Meren said, setting his cup down quickly. "Why didn't you say so? We have to find them."

"Nonsense. Press a little harder, Mistress Anath. Ah, yes. That's the spot where the fiend is trying to bore a hole through my skull."

"Taharqa," Meren ground out, his patience gone.

"Listen, my friend. They should be back tomorrow. If they aren't, then we can look for them. Or rather, you can. I'm not trotting off into the desert. Now run along and let my servants tend to you. I must take my afternoon nap, and then we'll have the evening meal. I've sent for dancers from my tribe. You'll like them."

The next day came and went with no sign of Sebek or Meren's charioteer. Meren prowled Taharqa's compound and cursed himself for not hurrying south, even though there was no certainty that Sebek would be there when he arrived. The following morning saw Meren in the street with his chariot preparing to set out with guides and his men when an old man in a dusty kilt and headcloth appeared in the company of his charioteer. The two trudged wearily down the road, slowly closing the gap between them and Meren. The charioteer saluted, and his parched lips moved with difficulty.

"Lord, this is the one called Sebek, whom you seek. We would have been here sooner, but we encountered a small party of Nubian raiders. The garrison escorts ran them off."

Anath stepped into the street, heard this and asked, "What escort?"

"I provided a letter to the garrison commander asking his

assistance," Meren said. He turned to the charioteer. "Excellent work." He handed the old man a leather water bottle and motioned for another to be provided to the charioteer. "Abu, see that they are fed. Then bring Sebek to me in my chamber."

Meren watched Sebek walk slowly into the compound, then motioned to one of his men. "This interview will be recorded. Send Intef. He's not as quick at recording as Bek, but he's accurate."

"What are you doing?" Anath appeared at his side as he headed for the house.

"Preparing to question Sebek, of course."

"But a formal interview might endanger him."

Meren stopped on the front steps and regarded Anath solemnly. "Anath, my sweet, Sebek will be in danger until he talks to me. After that, he'll be much safer because it will be too late to prevent him from revealing whatever it is that the evil one wishes to conceal. You know this."

"Oh, I suppose you're right. It's just that I trust no one, not even your famous charioteers."

Glancing around to make sure no one was watching them at the moment, Meren bent down and kissed her on the forehead. "You're worried about me, aren't you?"

"I'm not certain I care for this ability of yours to read my heart," Anath said with a wry smile.

"Fear not," Meren said. "This drinker of blood has tried many times to get rid of me and failed. I'll wager he's stopped trying."

Anath gave him a disgusted look and continued up the steps. "Meren, I'm the Eyes of Babylon. Please don't say fatuous things to me."

He watched her progress, the curve of her hips as they moved beneath the dark blue of her shift, the gold-brown smoothness of her bare arms. "Forgive me," he called with a note of amusement in his voice. "I forgot to whom I was speaking."

She didn't answer or turn around. Meren grinned and followed her inside. A little over an hour later he was seated in his chamber beside Anath when Sebek was escorted into the room. The old man must have had close to six decades. His silver hair was close-cropped to frame a face like a brooding jackal. He had the superior height of his Nubian mother, but his skin was like the Black Land after it lay beneath the summer sun—faded brown and parched. Deep furrows lined his brow and formed crevices that went from his nose to the outside corners of his mouth. Yet despite these signs of age Sebek's body was well muscled. His body had not begun to sink in on itself as many did with age.

Meren accepted Sebek's humble greeting. Anath remained silent and watchful.

"Finding you has been difficult," Meren said.

"I beg forgiveness, lord."

"It is recorded that you received a grant of land near Heliopolis, but you never went there. Why is that?"

Sebek glanced around the room at the charioteer who was serving as scribe, at the guards who stood beside the door, at Anath. Meren watched as a familiar shuttered look passed over the old man's face.

"I found that I missed my homeland, lord."

Meren rose, causing Sebek to bow his head. He drew near the old man and said quietly, "Come with me." He crossed the room to the farthest corner, out of earshot of anyone. Sebek stood before him with his gaze lowered. "Lift your gaze, Sebek." When the guard looked directly at him, he went on. "I have come about the death of the great royal wife Nefertiti, the justified. I think you know why."

Sebek's eyes widened, but he remained silent.

"Sebek, I have a great deal of patience, but in the last few months I've nearly been killed several times and the experience has made me irritable and impatient. Therefore I will be more direct than is my custom. I have discovered that Queen Nefertiti did not die of the plague as was thought. She was poisoned." He stopped at the garbled sound that came from Sebek.

"By all the gods of Egypt, I knew it!" the old man said in a low, urgent voice.

Chapter 10

Gratification flooded Meren. At last he'd found someone who'd witnessed the events surrounding the queen's death and had lived to speak of it.

"Pharaoh, may he live in health and prosperity, has ordered me to pursue her killer, and this I will do. I must know what you know, and you must tell me quickly, for the evil one responsible for her majesty's death has great power. He has killed many to preserve his secret. If he knew I wanted to speak to you, he'd have killed you. Your safety lies in telling me everything you know. Once you've spoken, there is no profit in killing you."

Sebek wet his lips. "I . . . never knew for certain what happened, lord. To speak against great men, it is impossible for a low one such as I."

"Sebek, I haven't time for your humility. Pharaoh commands that you speak."

"Yes, lord."

Meren nodded and returned to his chair. Sebek sat on the floor facing him. Meren glanced at Intef, who was sit-

ting cross-legged on the floor with a sheet of papyrus
stretched over his kilt. The charioteer dipped his rush pen
in black ink.

"Regnal year five," Meren began. "Under the Horus of
Gold, Who Elevates the Crowns and Satisfies the Gods,
King of Upper and Lower Egypt, Nebkheprure, Son of Ra,
Tutankhamun, given life." He glanced at the scribe. "Write
the date, Intef, and say, 'On this day, thus testifies the guard
Sebek before Meren, hereditary prince, the Eyes and Ears
of Pharaoh.'"

Meren inclined his head at Sebek. "Begin as you will,
and speak of the events surrounding the illness of the great
royal wife, Nefertiti, justified."

Sebek glanced around the room at Meren, at the charioteer serving as scribe, the others beside the door, and finally at Anath. His brow wrinkled as he beheld her, and
he almost spoke, but seemed to think better of it. Turning
his gaze back to Meren, Sebek cleared his throat and em-
barked upon his testimony.

It was year fourteen of the reign of the pharaoh Akhenaten,
the heretic. The day the queen fell ill I was standing guard outside her rooms, waiting for her majesty to appear for a great
reception. This was after pharaoh had scandalized the whole of
the Two Lands by making the great royal wife king at his side.
Such a thing had not been done before, to make a wife king
while pharaoh lived. All of us were amazed.

I remember the confusion among us guards. How were we
to conduct ourselves before a woman who was a king? I puzzled over this, prayed to Amun to guide me—secretly, because,
of course, to pray to Amun was forbidden. The god did not
answer, and I could tell that her majesty's heart was full of

confusion too. For a full day after pharaoh told her what he planned she kept to her rooms and refused all nourishment.

Finally the priest Thanuro came to us bearing instructions from the minister Tutu. We were henceforth guards of a king. The ceremonies and rights of a pharaoh were to be performed for the great royal wife. Such orders did nothing to dispel our confusion, for a king is a man. That is what the word means. How can a woman be a king?

We did as we were ordered. Pharaoh's word was accomplished, but we were unhappy. Queen Nefertiti was great of heart, a defender of order, harmony, and the old gods. Her dismay failed to ebb as the days passed.

On the morning of the great reception of the viceroy the queen—I must call her so, for that is what she would have wished—the queen was agitated. A guard hears things, you understand, and I was there when she spoke of her reluctance to appear yet again in the raiment of a king. Her hands shook, and she was flushed. She even raised her voice to her women, something she hardly ever did. She refused to eat until one of the noble ladies, one who was a close friend, persuaded her to sample a dish of lamb in a dill sauce. The queen complained of a queasy stomach, and sent for her physician. The physician gave her a tonic, but her majesty found it bitter and didn't finish it.

After an hour of ministration the queen felt able to dress. I was outside her bedchamber while she readied herself for the ceremony. At last she appeared. It was a sight I will never forget, for she seemed aflame. Her eyes glittered with the brightness of Ra, and her skin was as red as carnelian. Her neck seemed too fragile to hold up the double crowns of a pharaoh, and she swayed slightly as she walked.

The Lord Meren was there when she entered the audience chamber and collapsed. Many were there. We carried her majesty back to her bedchamber and summoned the royal physicians. They stared and poked and mumbled. Then they gathered in a corner like a flock of pigeons and fumbled with medical scrolls and argued.

Meanwhile I sent a guard to pharaoh's quarters and set more men around the queen's rooms to make sure no one came in who didn't belong there. Her women tried to persuade her to take an infusion ordered by the physician, but all the queen would take was water.

Days passed during which her majesty seemed to get better only to grow worse. When she improved, her women could persuade her to take food. There was a little maid, a favorite of the queen's, who could always convince her to eat a small meal in the morning. Until she grew worse. Once the plague took hold for good, the queen ordered herself moved to the smaller palace where she wouldn't be a danger to pharaoh and her daughters.

My men grew afraid, but I told them if anyone tried to leave, I would kill him. The great royal wife had been good to us, given us increased rations to feed our families, sponsored our sons in the army and navy, given rich gifts at births and marriages. She defended us against complaint and interference. When had any of us served such a mistress? The queen even sent her physician to my wife when she was dying. Never has there been such a queen.

And so we stayed. Some of her women were afraid to attend her. They pretended to be sick to escape the duty. Most remained, though, even when it was clear that the queen would die. The weaker the queen grew the fewer people she received. She sent Prince Tutankhamun away as soon as she became ill. The priest Thanuro annoyed the queen, always had, and she refused to see him at all.

I remember how hard it was to stand guard. To see the pa-

rade of physicians dwindle as hope faded. The palace was filled with whispers and chants against disease demons.

Two days before she died the queen summoned me and ordered her bed carried into the sunken garden. My men and I obeyed and set the bed between two columns facing the greenery. The queen smiled at the sight of the poppies and cornflowers growing there, and one of the women started crying. The laborers crept around the garden watering the flower beds and weeping silently.

The next day a noblewoman sent a dish prepared by her own hand, but the great royal wife was too ill to do more than taste it. Prince Usermontu came several times from pharaoh to inquire after her majesty. The last time he stayed but a moment and hurried away. Then pharaoh came, and we remained on duty throughout the night. The maids said that the queen had sunk into a stupor from which no one could wake her, not even pharaoh. We knew then that her end approached.

I was almost asleep on my feet early the next morning when a great wail startled me. I rushed into the queen's chamber and saw the living god throw himself across the body of the great royal wife. Lord Ay was holding the queen's hand. He just sat there staring at nothing while pharaoh wept. Suddenly the king rose up over her, threw back his head, and bellowed like a fiend of the underworld. Then Prince Usermontu came in and shouted at me to leave. Soon after that the priest Thanuro appeared with a company of pharaoh's guards and dismissed the queen's guards. I never saw the queen again.

A long silence filled the room after Sebek finished speaking. Meren watched Intef's pen brush across the papyrus, listing the names of the witnesses.

"A good accounting," he said. "And now, Sebek, I have

questions. The first I think you already expect. Do you know who poisoned the great royal wife Nefertiti?"

When Meren asked the question all movement in the room ceased. Intef's pen froze in the middle of a word. The other charioteers hardly blinked, and Anath became still.

"No, lord," Sebek said. "I don't know who might have poisoned the great royal wife."

Meren studied the old man. Sebek had been Nefertiti's most trusted bodyguard. The great Queen Tiye had appointed him. Meren knew he'd gone everywhere with Nefertiti. But Sebek had retired as soon as he could after the queen died. He hadn't transferred to another royal household even though he would have been welcome. Tutankhamun had a great affection for those who had served Nefertiti well, and Sebek would have been assured a high place under the boy king.

Sebek's voice vibrated with emotion when he spoke of Nefertiti. The queen had liked and trusted the guard, who had not been afraid to tell her the truth when asked. Sebek's story was the truth, Meren decided, but not the complete truth. As he watched the old man Meren toyed with the wide band of gold on his wrist. Hinged so that it formed two curved halves, the bracelet was inlaid with crystal and amethyst. His fingers stilled, then he lifted his hand and signaled to Abu.

"This interview is concluded."

The charioteers left, and Sebek rose to go as well.

"Sebek, remain here," Meren said. He turned to Anath, who had been quiet throughout the questioning. "I must speak with this man alone."

"Really, Meren. Why did you bring me to Egypt if you won't allow me to help you?"

"You've been of great assistance; and will be again. But I must do this without your help."

Anath left, giving Sebek a hard look as she went. Abu stepped out of the room and shut the door. He would remain with two charioteers just outside. Meren rose and went to Sebek, who bowed and lowered his gaze to the floor.

"Hear me, Sebek." Meren came close and lowered his voice. "There are guards at the door, on the roof, and below the windows outside. No one can hear. Do you understand?"

"Yes, lord."

"Then I ask again. Do you know who caused the queen's death?"

"No, lord."

Meren stared at the old man's set features. Then he lifted his wrist and pushed back the heavy bracelet to reveal the sun disk Akhenaten had ordered branded into his flesh.

"Look at this. You know what the heretic did to me, and you know the queen trusted me. You and I have shared danger together when the great royal wife and her father met with the priests of Amun." He unfastened his beaded belt and opened his overrobe to reveal the scar in his side. "The evil one seeks my death, because I won't stop until I find him." Meren let the ends of the robe fall loose. "You may speak freely, without fear that your words will be used against you. I swear by the ka of our beloved queen, I will never betray you."

Sebek's body seemed to lose its rigidity. He let out a long breath and sagged.

"It's true, lord, we risked our lives to serve her, you and I, but it has been a long time, and I didn't know if you'd changed. Forgive me."

"I would have done the same in your place," Meren said. "Now tell me everything."

"She fell ill too suddenly for my taste," Sebek said. "I didn't believe the physicians, but who was I to question them? So I watched when her food and drink were brought. I saw nothing."

"The steward gave the cook the poison to mix in the kitchen," Meren said. "Who could have caused Wah to do such a thing? Think, Sebek. Who were Wah's confidants?"

"I can think of several. Lord Pendua, Prince Usermontu, Thanuro, one or two of her highborn ladies, perhaps. But the ladies who befriended the steward have died."

"What of the men?"

Sebek scratched his head. "Pendua and Thanuro wanted power and riches. So did Usermontu. They all did, and Wah sought their company to further his own career. But Usermontu was different, because he was also mean. He would have killed out of hate because the queen forced him to stop maltreating his wife.

"I remember seeing him talking in corners with the steward," Sebek said. "If anyone came close, they would stop speaking until they were alone again. Usermontu wasn't respected by any of us in the army. No one respects a man who beats his wife. Even worse, he hadn't the courage to challenge a man. We all knew he ran from fights with his equals. When she learned Usermontu also kicked his children, the queen ordered them taken away and given to their mother. She couldn't hide her contempt. I remember her saying he treated the royal horses better because he knew she and pharaoh would have him executed if he hurt them."

"And he was around when the queen was sick," Meren said.

"Yes, lord. If she'd lived, I believe her majesty would have convinced pharaoh to banish him."

"What of Pendua and Thanuro?"

"Pendua was a place-seeker who used his position to enrich himself. When he was in charge of the queen's traders he exacted tolls from them in exchange for the best assignments. He aspired to high office and refused to see that he lacked an intelligent heart that would gain him royal favor. Servility and bribery were his tools. In truth, lord, I cannot imagine Lord Pendua as a master of great plots. He's a petty little man who sees no further than his fingers can grasp. Now that I think of it, he, Wah and Usermontu were like a pack of hyenas in the household. If one of them scented trouble, he would howl and bring the rest."

Sebek shook his head. "Now, Thanuro, he was different."

"Why?"

"The queen could never decipher him. She knew he spied on her for the king, reported actions of hers that might be interpreted as a betrayal of the Aten. There were times when she thought he suspected she was meeting with the priests of Amun, yet he never went to pharaoh with his suspicions. Perhaps she was wrong."

"But you don't think so."

Sebek rubbed his chin. "I could never understand Thanuro either. Pharaoh didn't know it, but he spent more time accounting for tithes and levies than in worship of the Aten. He would recite the prayers and hymns to the sun disk, but his zeal vanished when he thought himself unobserved. And he liked the company of odd sorts, for an Aten priest."

"What do you mean?"

"He favored the company of foreigners and some of the more disreputable nobles. But most of the time he was watching the queen. Still, her majesty knew about him and prevented him from doing much harm."

Meren wrapped his overrobe around his waist and refastened his belt. "I'm also interested in a merchant called Dilalu, who sold horses to the queen."

"Yes, he was at the palace frequently. Usermontu dealt with him, took bribes from him most likely. He was making a fortune until the queen discovered his other activities. She was going to speak to pharaoh about him. He might have ended up in a crocodile pit if she hadn't died."

"Exactly," Meren said. "And what of an Asiatic called Zulaya?"

"Zulaya. In truth, lord, I've never heard of a man by that name."

"During her last days, did you see anything strange, see anyone interfere with the queen's food or drink?"

"No, lord. If I had, I would have reported it immediately. I was vigilant, but finally I convinced myself that I was so grieved at her illness that I wanted to blame someone I could punish instead of an invisible disease demon."

"But you're certain that Usermontu and Pendua were close confidants of Wah, and that they as well as Dilalu had reason to fear the queen and do her harm."

"Yes, lord. Of all those close to the queen during her illness, they are the most likely to have committed this great evil."

"You can think of no others who might have had the power and the opportunity to cause her death?"

"No, lord. As I said, I finally had to accept that the plague took her. Still, I was desolate that so kind and great a lady had been struck down. All I had were vague suspicions. Indeed, I began to think I must have imagined a plot against her majesty, perhaps because I was privy to the dangerous tasks she was performing. In any case, to remain in royal service would have been to remain among those who had wished her ill. That I couldn't bear, so I retired."

"But why did you not remain on the land granted to you?"

"Because, lord, I am a careful man. I noticed that many who had served the queen met with fatal accidents or died during the months after her death. If some evil was at work, I wanted to escape it."

Meren placed his hand on the man's shoulder. "You are a wise man, Sebek, and you've done well."

"I am grateful, lord."

"Should you remember anything else, you must tell me. If I'm gone, tell Prince Taharqa, and he will send to me. Meanwhile, I think it best that you remain here."

"But my animals, lord, I must—"

"The prince will make arrangements for your household. I don't think you're in danger anymore, but to be certain you should stay here until the evil one can no longer do harm."

"But that could be a long time, lord."

"I don't think so," Meren said. Sebek gave him an inquiring look, but he didn't explain himself.

Indeed, Meren didn't know why he felt time was short. He was getting that burning sensation in his chest. He'd missed something or failed to recognize the meaning of something. The knowledge, whatever it was, lurked just beyond cognition, a faint shadow inside his ka, flitting across the terrain of his heart without leaving footprints.

He dismissed Sebek and settled into his chair once more. He was frustrated that he couldn't make himself understand or remember whatever it was that eluded him. He shifted in his chair as the burning in his chest grew, and jumped when Anath shoved the door open and sailed into the room.

"Well?"

"Nothing, curse it. Oh, he knew more about the people we already suspect, but nothing new."

"Unfortunate," she said as she dropped onto a cushion by his leg. She draped an arm over his thigh.

"He seemed to suspect Prince Usermontu more than anyone else. Called him mean."

"Usermontu has a reputation for mean-spiritedness and viciousness."

"It hasn't come to my attention lately."

Anath nodded. "I'm sure he's careful not to attract your notice."

"He has now," Meren said. "They all have, and it's time to let them know."

"What do you mean?"

"We're going home, and when we get there, I'm going to question each of them. The time for discretion has passed. I don't think I'll learn anything else of import until we force them to talk. From what Sebek has told me I can start with Pendua and Usermontu. By now Kysen has already questioned Dilalu."

"Good."

Meren shook his head. "Not good. Questioning two noblemen, even at the command of pharaoh, is risky. Prince Usermontu and Lord Pendua might not hold government office, but they're related to some of the most powerful families in Egypt. Usermontu's lineage is connected to the royal treasurer Maya's, and Lord Pendua is cousin to the high priest of Ptah. Lesser actions have been the source of great evil in the past. If Pendua's family is shamed, his whole lineage will blame me. They might even blame pharaoh. And should they suffer adversely, lose estates and power, they will seek out other malcontents and perhaps foster rebellion. Small feuds, my sweet, contain the seeds of civil war."

"But not if you're careful," Anath said with a pat to his thigh. "I know you. You'll manage it well."

"But can I get to the truth without destroying the harmony and balance of Egypt?"

"You've accomplished many difficult tasks for pharaoh. You can do this. It will be perilous, but you've had much experience that will serve you well." She smiled at him.

Meren smiled back. It was a relief to be able to speak to a woman about his difficulties, but his smile faded. "I'm going to talk to Zulaya too."

"Why? He wasn't even at Horizon of the Aten."

"No one saw him," Meren said, "but that doesn't mean he wasn't there."

"You know that's unlikely. Besides, it will waste time. You told me how important it is to finish this business for pharaoh's sake. It's more likely that the evil one we seek is an Egyptian, not some unimportant foreign merchant."

"Ah, but I have another reason for wanting to confront him. I met him once, although he doesn't know it. I was in disguise at the time. Zulaya's not an ordinary merchant. He latched on to me at once despite my changed appearance, and I want to know why. I want to know why he's so elusive, and why he seems to live nowhere in spite of his having great riches. Even if he had nothing to do with Nefertiti's death, he's hiding something."

"Have someone else investigate him, then. You needn't do it yourself when your attention should be fixed on more important questions. I'll do it if you insist on it being done."

"No," Meren said gently. "I thank you, but I will attend to it myself."

"But—"

"I said no. Zulaya wants too badly to remain unobserved."

Sighing, Anath rose and leaned down to almost touch her lips to his ear and whispered, "There are many reasons a man might avoid the notice of the Eyes of Pharaoh, my love."

Meren turned his head and met Anath's amused eyes. Her breath was sweet as the north wind. It skimmed over his face and threatened to make him forget what he was going to say—almost.

"I agree, dear Anath. A man may have many reasons to avoid my notice, but none would be so compelling as having murdered a queen."

Chapter 11

The trip back to Memphis took over two weeks in spite of the swiftness of *Wings of Horus*. Meren stopped at Horizon of the Aten only long enough to pick up his men and found that the scribes had collected more boxes of documents but hadn't examined all of them. Then he sailed north again, adding the strength of his oarsmen to the powerful rush of the Nile's current.

The return voyage hadn't been as restful for either Meren or Anath. Meren's temper grew short with the realization that he hadn't made a great deal of progress. Nefertiti's murderer was still roaming free. Anath had tried to distract him by playing her lute and singing to him, by making him play long games of senet, and by telling him stories of the people she'd met in the northern empire and Babylon. Yet he still remained distracted and anxious, putting aside his worries only at night. Then he needed the strength of Montu, god of war, to keep up with Anath and respond to her creative inclinations. She teased him that he'd become entirely too proper and scrupulous.

"You're fortunate, Meren my love, that I came home when I did. Another year and you'd have ended up as rigid as the red granite of Syene."

"And you would have languished abroad for lack of an Egyptian consort worthy of you," Meren had replied, no longer disturbed by Anath's references to his reserved manner.

When the ship docked at the capital Meren followed Anath down the gangplank. Anath was wearing a red gown and a long gold belt that wrapped around her hips and hung down to her feet. A filigree headband of rosettes kept her wild hair out of her face. As they walked down the plank she glanced up at Meren, a slight smile on her lips.

"You needn't escort me home, you know. I have servants and guards enough to protect a royal princess."

"But you don't seem to know what is due to you as a lady of rank." Meren helped her step into his chariot. "You may know how to wring secrets out of Asiatic ministers, but you have little conception of decorum and protocol."

Anath poked him with her forefinger. "Are you saying I'm uncivilized?"

"I prefer to say unschooled in proper Egyptian etiquette."

"Meren, you're a foul toad. I know you, and I know what you're saying. You think I'm only half civilized and contaminated by foreign influence."

He grinned down at her. "A few months at home should cure you."

They set off with one charioteer preceding them as an escort. Having succeeded in provoking sparks of irritation in Anath, he argued good-naturedly with her most of the way to her house. It was on the outskirts of the foreign district in an area favored by traders from Cyprus and Byblos. Anath seemed weary, and Meren was anxious to go home and find out how Kysen's investigation was proceeding, so he took his leave after seeing her safely through the gate.

By the time he reached Golden House the sun had set. The compound sparkled with torchlight, and he heard lively music, the beat of drums and laughter. Kysen and Bener were entertaining. Meren stepped down from his chariot and handed the reins to a groom. People were walking around the twin reflection pools in front of the house and mingling on the loggia. He saw Prince Djoser and several of the daughters of the old king, Amunhotep the Magnificent, as well as Maya, the royal treasurer. Speaking briefly with each, he tried to maintain a pleasant demeanor in spite of his irritation. Kysen shouldn't be entertaining in his absence. The last thing Meren wished for after his long journey was a house party at which he would have to be charming.

He went inside and worked his way around the crowded reception hall. It was filled with luxuriously dressed aristocrats. Some lounged on couches and chairs, others lay on cushions on the floor while servants poured an endless stream of imported wine and domestic beer. The air was filled with the scent of spices and roasted meat. He couldn't see either Kysen or Bener. Kysen was most likely moving around the house making sure his guests were well fed and happy.

And Bener was probably in the kitchens directing food preparation; she wasn't as sociable as her sisters, and Meren was beginning to worry about her future. She seemed to have little inclination to marry, which wasn't natural. Women married and had children. They were the foundation of life, and without children who would provide for her in old age? Who would furnish food and drink for her spirit once she was dead? After he solved this murder, he resolved he would speak to her about her future.

Meren thought he glimpsed Kysen in one corner of the

room. He threaded his way through the guests but his
progress stopped at the wide, muscled back of a tall nobleman who reeked of frankincense and wine. He heard a
high, soft voice. Not a woman's voice, merely a high man's
voice. There was only one young man in Memphis with the
build of a wrestler and the voice of a temple chantress, and
that would be Lord Rudu, Usermontu's son. He was flirting with a painted and bejeweled young woman who had
her head half averted. She was giggling and simpering in a
most obnoxious manner. She plied a hand fan and even
tapped Rudu on the forearm with it. Meren spoke as she
began to purr and coo at the object of her blandishments.

"Lord Rudu," Meren said, hoping to get by with a nod.

Rudu turned. "Lord Meren, by the blessings of Amun,
you're home."

"Father!"

The painted and bejeweled simperer stuck her head around
Rudu's massive shoulder. Meren stared at Bener.

"Daughter?" he said faintly.

"You've returned," she said, swallowing hard and edging
around Rudu to touch Meren's cheek with hers in greeting.

"Yes, I've returned," Meren said. "At a most favorable moment, it seems."

"Indeed, Lord Meren." Now Rudu was simpering. He tit-
tered at Meren and inclined his head. "A most favorable moment, would you not agree, Bener my little bean goose?"

Bener dragged her gaze from Meren. "What? Oh. Yes, my
great warrior. We're blessed by Hathor."

Meren scowled at Rudu, then at his daughter.

"Lord Meren," Rudu piped. "Mistress Bener has invited
me and my father and mother to sail on your pleasure yacht
tomorrow. I hope you'll be there too."

Meren blinked at Rudu. The young fool was inviting him

aboard his own ship. The wine fumes and heavy scent coming from Rudu sparked an ache in Meren's head. A vein throbbed at his temple. Bener had no use for Rudu. She'd primped herself and wooed the idiot as some sort of scheme to investigate Prince Usermontu. If Usermontu really was guilty of murdering Nefertiti and discovered the ruse, he wouldn't hesitate to kill both Kysen and Bener.

Gritting his teeth, Meren managed a smile. "Alas, I'm too weary from my journey. Perhaps another time, Lord Rudu."

"Of course," Rudu replied.

Meren took Bener's hand and squeezed it firmly. "Bener, my dear, where is Kysen?"

Bener gave Rudu a nervous smile, tugged her hand out of Meren's, and pointed to a group of chairs on the other side of the master's dais. "Over there, Father."

Meren politely excused himself, gave a severe look to Bener, and joined a group of men sitting in a small circle around a table laden with wine flagons and food. Kysen was one of them, and sitting to his right was Prince Usermontu looking as pleased as if he'd received the Gold of Honor from pharaoh. Meren greeted the two and nodded to Maya, General Horemheb, and the royal high steward, Amunhotep. A slave brought Meren's chair from the dais, and he sat between Usermontu and Maya.

The prince had never been a modest man. He had a commanding air and attitude of entitlement that had always irritated Meren. His sharp gaze spoke of a calculating intelligence. Of middle stature, with drooping eyelids and the remnants of pleasing looks that had once fascinated court ladies, Usermontu had aged since his days of influence at Horizon of the Aten. He'd developed a tremor in his hands that he concealed by keeping them clasped, but he seemed in great good humor this evening.

"I saw you come in, Meren," said Usermontu. "I'm glad you're back, because something of great import has happened in your absence."

Meren raised his eyebrows at Kysen, who was abnormally silent. His son barely met his gaze before looking down at the cup of wine in his hands.

"What might that be?" Meren asked.

Usermontu beamed at him. "Can't you guess? You were speaking with my son and your daughter not a moment past."

Meren turned and looked at the two young people. Bener leaned up to Lord Rudu and laughed as she swished her transparent overrobe and tossed her elaborate false tresses. Her lashes fluttered, and Rudu's chest swelled.

Looking down to conceal his horror, Meren cleared his throat and straightened in his chair. "I see. Indeed, this is a surprise. A pleasant one, to be sure, but one best discussed privately. I'm sure you agree, prince."

Usermontu gave him a look of knowing familiarity that made Meren want to cuff him. The man was a brute to women, and Meren had never invited him to Golden House because he detested such barbarity. Now here he was wallowing in the reception hall, smirking. And he had the presumption to think that Meren would— Best not pursue that thought.

"Kysen," Meren said lightly. "I would have a word with you regarding family business." He rose and bowed to the guests. "You understand, my friends. Matters that can't be delayed after so long an absence."

Maya gave him a sly look. "Naturally. I'm sure there are things that have come up that are quite urgent."

"Urgent," Horemheb repeated with a grin that turned into a laugh.

Sending a scowl in their direction, Meren left with Kysen on his heels. He sought the comparative privacy of a dark corner behind three tall jars of beer in stands. Rounding on Kysen, he hissed.

"Explain yourself, my son."

Kysen winced and said with a rush, "I'm sorry, Father. Bener began this little play of hers without consulting me. I came upon her hanging over the roof ledge goggling and simpering at Rudu, and the next day he was in our garden. He loafed there half the day with Bener, and after he left, I told her she couldn't invite him here anymore. But she had already asked him again. She said Prince Usermontu was ecstatic with anticipation at the possibility of a match between her and his son. After that, I couldn't think of a way to get out of the situation without offending the prince, so I decided to wait until you came back."

"I cannot believe this," Meren muttered.

He collected his thoughts while Kysen eyed him with anxiety.

"This whole pretense was unnecessary, curse it. I'm going to begin open questioning of Usermontu, Lord Pendua, and Dilalu. Has Bener learned anything?"

"I don't know," Kysen said unhappily. "She's says she's too busy to talk, but I think she's been avoiding me."

"She won't be busy much longer," Meren snapped.

Kysen sighed and said, "I might as well tell you she also visited Lord Pendua's wife."

Meren stared at him open-mouthed. "By the gods, Ky. I have to be able to leave without you two mismanaging my affairs."

Kysen nodded, his half-moon eyes sad. "I have failed you."

Relenting, Meren clapped him on the shoulder. "It's not so bad. Bener is difficult, and you're easygoing."

Looking past Meren, Kysen pointed. "I may be, but Lord Irzanen isn't."

Meren turned to see one of his newest charioteers lurking near Bener and Lord Rudu. He'd noticed Irzanen's interest in Bener, and it was apparent that the young man took offense at Rudu's attentions to Bener. He directed knifelike looks at his rival through eyes narrowed to slits. He prowled around the two, moving from group to chattering group, craning his neck and muttering to himself. If the room hadn't been so crowded he would have attracted attention.

Meren sighed and started for the young charioteer. "At least Irzanen is from a family of decent character. I know you think he's too trusting."

"He's simple," Kysen said as he followed Meren to where Irzanen stalked his unsuspecting quarry.

"Not simple. You mistake his straightforward manner and lack of diplomacy for stupidity." Meren slowed and came to a stop in the middle of the hall. "What is this?"

A long line of servants approached from the anteroom, each carrying a basket or some other burden. As they snaked their way toward Meren they nudged, bumped, and shoved guests with their burdens. At their head was a short, squat man with a bumptious manner and jewelry too big for his small frame.

"Pendua," Meren said in disbelief.

Kysen groaned. "I forgot Bener had invited him."

Lord Pendua marched up to Meren, his chest stuck out, his head held as high as it would go. He beamed at his hosts like a great general returning from a victory against the wild tribes of Kush. Pendua was one of those men who made up for lack of height by acquiring great strength. He exercised so much that even his chin seemed muscled. Unfortunately all those muscles made him seem wider rather than taller, giving him a simian appearance. When he walked he bounced on the balls of his feet as if he expected to be attacked and would be disappointed if he wasn't.

Indeed, among his equals Pendua was always ready for fights that seldom developed. He had a quick temper, and a habit of overdoing whatever he attempted. Meren looked askance at the dozens of servants crowding the hall and resigned himself. Nodding when Pendua bowed to him, he gave Kysen a covert glare and welcomed his guest.

"May Ra shine favorably upon your house, Lord Meren." Pendua glanced around the room to make sure everyone had stopped talking and was watching him. Then he proceeded. "I come to your feast bearing gifts of appreciation for the new friendship that has sprung up between the ladies of our households. Where is that servant? Oh, there you are. Well, come on, come on."

A serving man came forward with a square ivory box ornamented with gilded hieroglyphs symbolizing life and health. He lifted the lid to display sixteen compartments, each bearing a small gold or silver vessel.

Pendua indicated the box with a flourish. "For my dear friend, Lord Meren. Rare spices of Nubia and Punt." He beckoned to the next servant in line. "Three pistacia seedlings for your garden. Come along, all of you." The servants passed in quick succession while Pendua announced what they bore. "Cakes of ladanum resin for incense, six whole jars of fenugreek oil, four whole jars of colocynth oil, five whole jars of poppy oil, seven baskets containing dried chamomile, sweet flag, coriander, mint, thyme, and bryony."

"Pendua," Meren said.

"Alkanet shrubs, half a dozen bottles of the best cedar oil." Pendua held up something in his hand. "A pair of gilded leather sandals." He shoved them at a servant and grabbed a box from the next. "A set of throwing sticks of the finest polished cedar." He gave the box back to a servant and ignored Meren's attempt to interrupt him again. "Six pairs of fine driving gloves, a stool of gilded wood, ebony, and ivory, and an unguent vase carved in the likeness of an ibex."

Pendua rushed forward and snatched an object covered with a cloth and held it out to Meren. "And my last and greatest gift."

With great ceremony and pride, Pendua unveiled a vase of pure, shining silver in the shape of a pomegranate. A murmur of admiration went through the assembled guests. Meren looked at it in alarm, then hastened to thank Pendua before the man could launch into another speech. He called for wine for his guest and ushered him to the group sitting beside the master's dais. With Pendua ensconced in the best chair of ebony, cedar, and gold, he sat beside the man and beckoned to his son. Kysen came over and leaned down to hear him.

"I will avenge myself for this, Ky. Because of you and Bener I'm going to have to question this man after he has bestowed a small mountain of luxuries upon me. Go find your sister and tell her to bring this cursed feast to an end."

Meren forced himself to make conversation with Pendua and Usermontu. His real friends knew his opinion of the two men, so he endured knowing looks from Horemheb and glances of sly amusement from Maya. Finally Kysen returned, without his sister.

"Where is Bener?" Meren demanded under his breath as the conversation swirled around him.

"I can't find her."

"What do you mean you can't find her?"

"I've looked all over the house, sent the servants and charioteers to search the whole compound, asked everyone I met. She's gone."

"Nonsense."

Kysen dropped to one knee beside Meren and met his gaze with one of anxiety. "No, Father. That's why I took so long. We've searched everywhere. She's gone."

"In the middle of the feast," Meren said in a toneless voice.

The noise of the guests faded, and the room seemed to go dark. Bener had disappeared. She wouldn't run away from him out of fear. When she got into trouble, she faced his ire. Bener wouldn't leave an entertainment of which she was the hostess. She might have left in pursuit of something she perceived as a vital clue. Or someone forced her to go.

A cold, netherworld terror invaded Meren's heart. Only a lifetime's experience at hiding his feelings kept him in control, but barely. He went still, and all emotion faded from his expression.

"Bring Rudu and Irzanen to me at once. One of them has to know where she is."

"I've already talked to them, Father."

"One of them knows where she is," Meren repeated as he drummed his fingers on the chair arm. "They might not confide in you, but they're going to confide in me."

Chapter 12

Meren stilled the terror that made him want to summon his charioteers and rampage the entire city in search of his daughter. With a discipline learned at a court ruled by a dangerous fanatic he forced himself to remain in his chair conversing with his guests. It seemed an eternity before Kysen returned with Rudu and Irzanen.

"Ah, here's my son," Usermontu said with his habitual smirk. "The finest charioteer in the city. Can't think why you never admitted him into your company, Meren."

Ignoring the prince, Meren excused himself and walked over to a lamp stand with the three younger men. Rounding on them, he hissed. "Say at once where my daughter is."

"In truth, Lord Meren," Rudu said with a scowl at Irzanen. "You should ask this overgrown hyena pup here. He seems to think he has some interest in my connection with Lady Bener, which he does not. He appeared out of nowhere and blurted out the most foul accusations, and your daughter took offense."

Irzanen had been smoldering, and he uttered a curse. "You arrogant son of a—"

"Irzanen," Meren said in a quiet but lethal tone that silenced the charioteer. Having gained the attention of both men, he continued. "Tell me what happened after you had words before my daughter."

Irzanen cast a fulminating look at his adversary before he spoke. "I saw this—I saw him. He touched her face in front of everyone, the insolent dog. If you'd seen him, lord, you would have taken offense. I merely pointed this out to Lady Bener, but she became angry."

"Nearly snapped his nose off," Rudu said with a grin.

Kysen sighed. "No wonder I saw her drag Irzanen out of the reception hall."

"She was annoyed," Irzanen said reluctantly, reddening. "She pulled me outside, near one of the reflection pools in the front court, and berated me for interfering where I wasn't concerned. She—she's quite eloquent when she's angry."

Kysen asked, "Where did she go after your argument?"

"I don't know," Irzanen said. "She made me angry, accusing me of rudeness and calling me an officious busybody. I gave her a few of my own observations about her character, and then I left. I saw her stalking off toward the rear of the house as I went in the front door."

Meren held up his hand for silence. "Ky, you've searched the outbuildings and the gardens thoroughly?"

Kysen gave a sharp nod.

"You can't find her?" Rudu asked. He turned on Irzanen. "What have you done with her?"

Irzanen raised his fists and moved only to find Meren blocking his way. Meren's gaze cut into him, slicing through flesh and bone. His fingertips caressed the hilt of the dagger in his belt. Then Kysen was beside him.

"No, Father."

"Lord, I swear, I would never harm your daughter. I lo—
I admire her above all other women." When Meren said
nothing, Irzanen rushed on. "You may ask Mistress Takhat
or Prince Djoser. They saw her leave me, and they saw me
go inside alone."

Irzanen sighed with relief when Meren nodded and released him from his gaze. Meren hadn't really believed Irzanen responsible for Bener's disappearance, but he had to be
sure. Now there was no choice but to accept that his daughter was missing. The terror he'd been keeping at bay flared
up and intensified. He thought furiously while Kysen, Rudu,
and Irzanen argued the next step among themselves. Meren
cut through their exchange.

"Kysen, find Abu and tell him to seal the house and
grounds. No one is to leave . . ." His words faded away as
he saw Wia, his grandson's nurse, approaching. She held
something that made his heart pound against his chest. "Your
pardon, lord, but someone asked me to give you this."

In both hands she held dozens of beads that had once
been strung together, amethyst and gold ball beads inter-
spersed with tiny gold scarabs. He recognized them at once;
they'd formed a double-stranded necklace that had once been
his wife's. He'd given it to Bener last year at the Feast of
Opet. Wia dropped the torn necklace into Meren's cupped
hand. He barely heard Kysen swear as the nurse proffered a
folded and sealed note. Meren handed the necklace to Kysen,
broke the plain seal, and opened the note.

*Lady Bener is safe as long as you do as you are commanded.
Abandon at once the inquiry in which you are engaged. Go to
pharaoh and place responsibility for the crime upon Yamen. Let*

*none suspect your distress. Do as you are commanded by sun-
set tomorrow or your daughter will perish.*

The black spider's tracks that formed the script blurred
as Meren stared at the unsigned message. He made a guttural sound as a windstorm of fear and rage nearly consumed him. Rudu stepped back as Meren crushed the papyrus
and uttered a stream of brutal invectives.

Kysen moved between Meren and Rudu. "Forgive us, Lord
Rudu. No doubt my sister has been imprudent and has sent
a note to explain herself to Lord Meren. Please excuse us."

Meren closed his eyes and willed himself into silence as
Kysen ushered Rudu away. Then he opened his eyes and
sought out Usermontu. The prince was still chatting with
Pendua, Horemheb, and Maya and looking pleased with himself. Pendua was casting covert glances around the reception
hall as if looking for someone. Hatred flooded Meren. One
of them could be responsible for Bener's abduction. He could
find out. All he needed to do was dangle them from their
heels over a hungry crocodile on the riverbank. Meren narrowed his eyes, seething with the urge to attack.

"Lord?" Irzanen hovered beside him.

Meren ignored him, stared at Pendua, breathing hard.
Kysen appeared in front of him, and he barely felt the hand
on his arm.

"Father?" he whispered. "What is it?"

"He took her," Meren said, still staring. "Someone took
Bener."

When Kysen went mute Irzanen asked, "Who, lord?"

"Never mind," Meren said distractedly.

"But, lord!"

"Be silent!" Meren roared.

There was sudden quiet in the hall as guest after guest

paused. Meren darted glances around the room, then muttered to Kysen. "I'm going to my rooms. Tell them I'm ill. Tell them I'm still weak from my wounds, anything. End this damnable feast and get rid of everyone, but make sure you know who was here."

Without another word Meren shoved Irzanen aside. As he left someone stepped in his path.

"Not like you to lose your temper with one of your young recruits, old friend." Horemheb blocked his way, his eyes holding curiosity and faint worry.

Meren managed a wry smile. "I beg your forbearance. I seem to have taxed my strength without realizing it."

"By Amun, I knew it." Horemheb took Meren's arm before he could protest and waved away several friends who were converging on them. "Not now, not now. He's overestimated his endurance, the stubborn fool. Not as strong as he thought he was."

Meren almost objected, then took advantage of Horemheb's mistake. He leaned heavily on his friend's arm. Allowing himself to be guided across the reception hall, he passed Usermontu deep in conversation with his son. The prince glanced at Meren with the hint of a smile playing about his lips. Was it a smile of secret triumph? Barely able to contain the urge to lash that smile off the prince's face, Meren was trembling with suppressed fury when Lord Pendua hurried up to him. Horemheb growled at him, and Maya came over, smoothly inserting himself between Meren and Pendua, and steered the guest in the opposite direction. Horemheb pulled Meren out of the hall, down a corridor, and shoved him into the anteroom that led to his bedchamber.

"I'll find Zar and send him to you," the general said. "You go to your bed and lie down or I'll put you there myself."

He followed Meren into the next room and watched until his friend was seated on the bed. "Good."

He slammed the door shut behind him, and Meren was alone. Springing off the bed, he flung himself across the room, hesitated, paced to the other side, crossed yet again. He knew he was behaving like pharaoh's pet leopard aroused by a threat, but he couldn't remain still. Muttering to himself he paced around the chamber and tried to bring his emotions under control.

Seldom had he been faced with danger to his children; he took great care that this was so. Kysen had run afoul of a murderer last year. That had been a nightmare. Bener had put herself in danger recently, but only briefly. Now he might lose her forever, and the thought was driving him near to madness. His hands shook, and his heart filled with a thousand nightmarish imaginings. He prayed to Amun to protect her and hissed obscene curses against her abductors. The feeling of helplessness was almost overpowering.

He stopped himself in the middle of the third cursing spell. "Stop this. You're only making the fear worse. Think, damn you."

"Lord?" His body servant, Zar, came into the room.

Meren hardly looked at him and continued to prowl. "Send Abu to me. Go!"

By the time the charioteer arrived Meren was standing beside a chest that held his daggers. With a polishing cloth he was rubbing the blade of a bronze weapon in intense concentration. It was the only way he could preserve his calm.

"The evil one we seek has abducted Bener," he said softly.

Abu sucked in his breath. "What are your orders?"

"Recall all the agents we've sent in search of information."

"All?"

Meren didn't look up from the whetstone and blade. "Send the orders at once, and make a great show of it. I want no one to be seen making inquiries of any kind. Put Hapimen in charge of the task." Meren set the blade and cloth aside and met Abu's eyes with a stare of blank flatness.

"Gather the charioteers, but quietly and with the greatest secrecy. Have them search the entire compound for signs of the abduction, especially the garden and service buildings. I doubt there's a trail to follow, but if there is, find me before you follow it. If there's no trail send the men out while it's still dark to hunt for her."

Meren drew closer to this man who had protected him ever since he could remember. "Abu, they mustn't be seen trying to find her. Bener's life may depend upon their ability to search in concealment."

Abu gave him a fierce look. "I swear, we'll be as shadows inside the darkness. None will mark our passing."

"If the evil one suspects I've set them on his scent . . ." Meren couldn't finish, and his eyes closed again as he tried to shut out images of horror. He felt Abu's hand on his shoulder.

"We will find her." He moved away.

Meren whipped around. "Wait." He started to pace again, then stopped to stare in anguish at the charioteer. "If he can reach into my house and take one daughter, he can reach the others, even my sister and brother. Is General Horemheb still here?"

"I saw him as I came to you."

"Bring him, then do as I've ordered."

"Very well."

"And Abu," Meren said.

"Yes, lord?"

"We don't have much time."

They regarded each other with dread. Abu had been with him when they found the bodies of the queen's cook and her husband and Yamen dying in a dark street from wounds suffered at the command of this murderer of queens. The one they sought bathed in blood as if it were sweet-scented water.

The rest of the night passed slowly for Meren, each moment an agony of wondering what was happening to Bener. He asked Horemheb to send contingents to guard various members of his family and begged him not to ask the reason for the request. His friend was annoyed that Meren couldn't confide in him, but he agreed. He heard from Kysen a report of what had transpired in his absence and marveled that he kept his sanity through the whole tale.

By the time the sun rose half the charioteers had returned empty-handed. As the morning progressed the others reported back with the same results, and midday saw the end of Meren's hopes. A lengthier search risked alerting the abductor. Kysen returned from a sweep of the outer city districts haggard and unhappy.

"Not a sign of her," he said as he dropped wearily to a cushion beside Meren's chair in his office on the second floor.

Meren had been attempting to review the documents found at Horizon of the Aten. Bek and Dedi were plowing through stacks of papyri. Kenro hunkered over a chipped clay tablet translating the wedge-shaped script of the Asiatics.

Running a hand through his hair Meren muttered, "I didn't think you'd find anything."

"Father, you're the color of sun-bleached linen. Have you eaten?"

"What? I don't know. I'm not hungry."

Kysen lowered his voice. "Will he release her unharmed?"

"Has he once shown mercy since we began this cursed inquiry?"

"I should have stopped her. This is my fault."

Meren reached down to place his hand on Kysen's arm. "No. It would have happened no matter what you did. The evil one has planned this maneuver for a long time."

"What are we going to do?"

Swallowing hard in spite of a dry throat, Meren straightened. "I'm looking at every scrap of information we've gathered, but I don't think I'm going to suddenly find a sign that will reveal the identity of the evil one. It could be Usermontu. He could have sat there eating and smirking at me while his men took Bener. It could be Pendua or Dilalu. It could be someone we haven't even considered yet, like Zulaya. The only one I'm sure couldn't have done it is Yamen."

"The murderer is desperate to attempt such a thing," Kysen said. "I should try to find Dilalu again. Perhaps he knows enough to lead us to our enemy." Kysen rose. "I'll change into my Nen clothing and go to the Caverns."

"Take Reia with you."

"I'm more likely to get answers alone."

Meren's voice crackled with irritation. "That wasn't a request, Ky."

"Yes, Father."

Once Kysen was gone Meren returned to the documents he was reviewing. He had difficulty keeping his attention on what he was doing and shutting out his fear for Bener. He was going through a collection of records from Horizon of the Aten. They dated from late in Akhenaten's reign, years fourteen through seventeen. Tutankhamun's middle brother, Smenkhare, had ruled for a brief two years before dying of an ague, and this was the fifth year of the young pharaoh's rule. In that short time so much had happened, and yet these documents revealed little of the turmoil and danger that had threatened Egypt.

Meren sifted through tallies of the herds of cattle dedicated to the Mansion of the Aten from year fourteen of Akhenaten. He read a tattered sheet giving permission to transfer slaves from the royal women's household in the Fayuum oasis to Horizon of the Aten in year sixteen. Another papyrus contained orders to transfer deeds to new owners like the royal princesses, the temple of the Aten, favored courtiers, and servants like the priest Thanuro, all dated year sixteen.

There was a list of traders who had been granted the privilege of dealing with the king's household that included Dilalu. Bek handed him a weapons supply list for one of the garrisons at a fort on the Ways of Horus that guarded the route from Canaan into Egypt. The official who sent the supplies was Usermontu; the merchant who furnished the weapons was Dilalu.

"What does this signify?" Meren asked.

Bek shook his head. "I don't know, lord."

Suddenly Meren heard a yelp outside the office door. The portal slammed open, and Anath strode into the room. Behind her the guard he'd posted was cradling his hand. Meren signaled to him to shut the door and handed the supply list to Bek.

"What did you do to my man?"

Anath smiled and held out a decorative pin with a sharp point that had been clipped to her yellow robe. "He told me I couldn't come in. He was offensive, but he's learned manners now."

"Forgive me, but I can't see you now."

Folding her arms, Anath eyed him. "What's wrong?"

"Nothing."

"You look as if you haven't slept. The shadows of the netherworld mark your eyes." She came closer, frowning. "Something has happened. The whole household is silent. Everyone is creeping about as if someone's died. What's wrong?"

"No," Meren said faintly, avoiding her gaze. "Please, Anath, you must excuse me. I'll see you later."

Anath studied him for a moment, then shrugged. "Very well. I'll visit Bener."

Meren jerked around, fists clenched. "No! Leave me alone. Go away." Behind him the scribes looked at each other, then eased out of the room.

Anath watched them go. She contemplated the closed door for a while before approaching Meren. Her hand closed over his, and it was all Meren could do not to shake it off and bellow at her. He wanted to rush into the streets and scream Bener's name, order pharaoh's army to surround the city and search it house to house. Instead he ground his teeth together so tightly his jaw ached.

"You might as well tell me what's happened, my love," Anath said with gentle firmness. "I'll find out anyway."

So, haltingly, with hard-won restraint, he related what had happened since he left her. When he finished he sank to the cushion Kysen had used and buried his head in his arms, using the chair seat as a prop. A long silence ensued, and he was grateful to Anath for knowing him well enough to allow him time to recover. He lifted his head and stared at the polished and gilded cedar chair back.

"The message commands me to blame Yamen for the queen's murder. I've thought long about it." He looked into Anath's sorrowful eyes. "I can't lie to the Golden One. I'll have to tell him the truth."

Anath was beside him instantly. She took his face in her hands and whispered to him.

"No, no, no, my love. Do as the evil one commands."

Eyes bright with unshed tears, Meren whispered back, "Don't you see? He's going to kill her anyway. My only chance is to find her before he does."

Anath dropped her hands, sat back on her heels, and regarded him with a tortured expression. "Surely not, my love. Surely he knows what you'll do if he kills Bener."

"That's just it," Meren said in a choked voice. "For once I face an enemy who doesn't seem to fear what I can do to him, and that may cost my daughter her life."

Chapter 13

Seeing his own fear mirrored in Anath's face, Meren got to his feet slowly, turned his face away, and closed his eyes. "May Amun help me."

Anath came to him and put her arms around him. "Oh, Meren, I'm so sorry." He felt a strange, sharp ache in his throat as she gently guided his head to rest on her shoulder. Anath's touch, her arms, her soft sympathy threatened to drive him to tears. He hadn't wept since he ceased to grieve for Sit-Hathor. He wouldn't do it now when Bener needed his strength. He straightened and stepped out of the circle of Anath's arms.

"I can't deceive pharaoh, and there's no need. His majesty will understand that we must refrain from this inquiry for a while, until Bener is safe and the evil one lulled into believing he's won."

"You of all people know what this drinker of blood is capable of doing should he discover your deceit. And he will find out what you've done." She threw up her hands. "Isn't Bener's life worth a small lie?"

Meren stared at her. "It isn't a small lie. It's a lie to the living god of Egypt, one that furthers the designs of a murderer."

"But the crime is an old one," Anath said. "Who is hurt by it now?"

"Pharaoh is hurt. All of Egypt was hurt by this crime, and if he can kill a queen, he can murder a king too. Don't you think I've been over this a thousand times since she was taken? Besides, if I lied to pharaoh he'd find out."

"He's only a boy, Meren. You can make him believe the lie."

Meren shook his head. "You wouldn't say that if you'd spent much time with him. He has the wisdom, guile, and ruthlessness of Thutmose the Conqueror, and he can enthrall and beguile whomever he wishes. Pharaoh knows many things before I do, and he'd find out I lied to him before two days had passed." Meren sat down in his chair again and rubbed his forehead wearily. "He must be told."

Anath sighed. "I fear for Bener. Dear, funny Bener, who's too shy to admit she likes that callow Lord Irzanen, who takes care of everyone and asks for nothing in return. How can you risk her life?"

Meren sprang to his feet so violently that the chair shot back and tipped over. He fought the wrath that nearly overwhelmed him, raking Anath with a hate-filled stare, his body trembling. Anath took a step backward.

"Get out," he said.

"You're furious because I might be right."

"Get out, Anath, or by Amun's staff, I'll toss you into the street myself."

Her eyes met his with an unblinking challenge, but after a few moments of searching his face, she walked out of the room without another word. When he was certain she was out of the house Meren left the office and went to his bedchamber where Zar helped him bathe and dress to go to the palace.

Meren ended up at the royal workshops near the temple of Ptah, for pharaoh had gone there to inspect the progress of the work on his new war chariot. The workshop was a long, low building with walled courtyards in which carpenters sawed and shaped the expensive imported wood used to form the body, shafts, pole, and wheels of chariots. Elsewhere workers cut the leather that fastened parts together, covered the body and wheels, and formed the reins and blinkers. There was another room devoted to the manufacture of whips.

Draped in transparent linen, gold, and carnelian jewelry and shod in fine leather sandals, Meren passed sweating carpenters' assistants. Several held a wooden chariot shaft while another jumped on it to test its flexibility. Beneath an awning of dried palm leaves a chariot master directed more assistants in binding wheel felloes. Walking around a stack of spokes, Meren entered the main workroom.

Tutankhamun was standing in the center of the workroom accompanied by the treasurer Maya, Karoya, and half a dozen royal guards. He was talking to the chief overseer and royal chariot master, who was showing off the body of the king's new vehicle. Of gessoed wood overlaid with gold, the compartment had been embellished with bands of precious stones and glass. The central panels were engraved with the wings of the solar falcon, which protected the names of the king and queen. The axle, wheels, shaft, and yoke were glossy black and inlaid with gold bands.

Meren approached and waited for Tutankhamun to notice him. He dreaded this interview, for he would have to admit helplessness, but he'd do anything to get Bener back.

Pharaoh stepped up into the chariot and bounced on the floor, testing the body's integrity. Meren noted with dread that he'd lost weight and seemed troubled even as he gripped the handrail, then leaned against it as he would while firing an arrow. Raising his arms as if he held a bow, he twisted his body while bracing his legs. As he turned he saw Meren, paused as their gazes touched. Something flickered in the king's eyes, but he continued his sweep with the imaginary weapon. Then he jumped to the floor, spoke a few words to the master, and waved his escort and Maya away. Craftsmen and courtiers filed out of the room, leaving Meren to come forward and kneel beside the gold-encrusted chariot.

"I heard you arrived last night," Tutankhamun said. The gold uraeus that held his headcloth in place caught a sunbeam from a window and flashed in Meren's eyes.

"Majesty, I beg leave to speak privately." Meren touched his forehead to the floor and sat up only to be startled when the king abruptly dropped to one knee close to him.

"What's wrong?" Tutankhamun's voice was low and urgent.

"Bener has been abducted. They took her last night after I came home." Meren pounded the floor, his voice rising. "While I was there, by all the demons of the netherworld!"

Alarm clear in his gaze, the king said, "Tell me what happened."

Meren took a deep breath and lowered his voice. He tried to speak without emotion, but by the time he finished, his body was tight with tension, while at the same time he felt as if he were looking at himself from a perch near the ceiling. It was as if his ka tried to take flight and search for Bener while his body remained earthbound, explaining to pharaoh.

Upon hearing Meren's words the king's expressive eyes filled with anger and sympathy. He stood and motioned for Meren to rise. "I knew something terrible had happened the moment I saw you." The king gripped the chariot rail hard and swore. "This insanity must end. I'll order everyone you suspect arrested and have them beaten with staves until one of them confesses."

"No, majesty!" Meren dropped to his knees again. "I beg you not to do this. I have no doubt that the evil one has given orders that Bener is to be killed should anything happen to him. We must be seen to comply with his commands."

Tutankhamun stared into Meren's pain-filled eyes, nodded, and lapsed into a thoughtful silence. Then he raised his gaze to Meren's once more. "It makes no sense, this attempt to force you to give up your search. Surely the evil one expects you to do as you propose, make a pretense of complying while secretly proceeding with your inquiries."

"Thy majesty is wise," Meren said. He drew an unsteady breath. "This abduction is more than it appears. It is a message to me. I am to understand that the evil one can harm me through my family at any time should he find it necessary."

"Can he?"

Meren looked away from the king's steady gaze. "Yes."

"Such power implies great wealth and cunning." Tutankhamun studied his heavy electrum signet ring. "Too much wealth, too much cunning. My majesty cannot allow such a subject to go free. You understand this, Meren."

"I do, Golden One."

"You have seen to it that the rest of your family are protected?"

"Aye, majesty."

Tutankhamun frowned. "You must have threatened him in some way for the evil one to resort to abduction."

"I've done little, majesty. I went to Horizon of the Aten, then to Syene to question the royal bodyguard Sebek. I think this abduction was planned after the evil one failed to ruin me in thy majesty's eyes. What I've learned of late isn't remarkable." Meren gave the king a report of his activities.

"Prince Usermontu, the two Asiatics, and Lord Pendua," pharaoh said. "I cannot imagine Pendua is the font of all this evil intrigue. He isn't known for his subtlety or the refined intelligence of his heart."

"Yet such a character would serve as excellent concealment for criminal activities. No one would suspect such a man." Meren shook his head and sighed. His head felt like it was stuffed with papyrus pulp. "Thy majesty's advisors were right to withhold favor from those whose avarice caused suffering under the old pharaoh. I've been reviewing a few records from the last years of the reign. Many of them had already received rewards of land, cattle, even gold in amounts far beyond any given for the kind of services they performed. Usermontu and Pendua certainly did. In fact, they were given more than most."

Tutankhamun ran a finger along the chariot's handrail. "What are you saying?"

"That Queen Nefertiti threatened to cut off their source of riches, and one of them might have killed her for it."

"Killing her did no good," the king said. "They lost their positions at court when I came to the throne."

"But the murderer couldn't have foreseen the death of Akhenaten and Smenkhare or thy majesty's actions."

Tutankhamun drew nearer and asked quietly, "What will you do now?"

"The hardest thing I have ever done, majesty. I shall do

nothing. It may drive me to madness." He flinched when the king put a hand on his arm and squeezed.

The touch of the living god conferred great honor and favor. It also provoked the enmity of jealous courtiers, but all Meren could think of was how useless his intimacy with the king was in the face of Bener's disappearance.

"My dear friend," Tutankhamun said in a low whisper. "I shall call upon my father Amun to protect you and Bener and all your family. I like your daughter. She can weigh hearts on the balance scale and isn't often fooled by liars or charlatans. She doesn't stare with her mouth open or titter and simper at me like so many noblewomen do."

Meren managed a brief smile. "She's the most practical and sensible of my daughters in many ways, but she isn't sensible about her proper sphere. It may have been her meddling in my affairs that provoked this abduction. She came to the evil one's attention by interfering in my investigation."

"It is unwise to allow women too much power, it's true." Tutankhamun's gaze grew unfocused, and Meren wondered briefly if he was thinking of Queen Ankhesenamun. He reflected painfully that Bener would disagree with their opinion.

"Not all women are as wise and clever as the great Nefertiti, majesty."

"I know," the king said.

"If thy majesty will permit, I will return to Golden House," Meren said.

"To do nothing."

"With elaborate care, my king."

"Very well," Tutankhamun said. "But, Meren, remember. This drinker of blood must be exposed and destroyed." He searched Meren's face and went on. "No matter the cost."

Meren felt his heart contract painfully. "Yes, Golden One. No matter the cost."

At home Meren did as he'd planned. He refused an invitation to a feast that arrived by messenger from the high priest of Ptah. When Maya arrived full of concern and curiosity to inquire after his health, he hid in his bedroom and protested his inability to receive visitors due to extreme fatigue. Out of sight in his office he conducted the business of the Eyes and Ears of Pharaoh, receiving royal messengers from all parts of the empire, studying reports from the city police of Memphis and Thebes, dispatches from the desert police, royal garrisons, the army and navy. He looked at dozens of papyri until he realized he was reading words without comprehending them, listening to heralds and messengers without hearing, signing documents without understanding them.

The hours crawled by, each moment made hideous with fear for his daughter. As night fell and the moon rose Kysen returned from the Caverns wearing that pungent mixture of odors characteristic of that area—beer, dust, and goat dung. Meren thought he caught a hint of the exotic perfume he connected to the Divine Lotus. Kysen wiped sweat from his brow, put his back to one of the columns in Meren's office, and sank to the floor with a sigh.

"Othrys has heard nothing about Bener. Neither have Ese or that wretch Tcha. Whoever took her has kept a closed mouth about it." Kysen's head listed backward, and he closed his eyes. "Dilalu's house is still deserted, but all his belongings remain. Tcha thought he glimpsed the bastard once near the docks, but he isn't sure how long ago."

"Tcha is a thief," Meren said as he signed the last of a series of letters and handed them to Bek. "He has no occasion to mark his days in any manner except by how much he's been able to steal."

"But at least we know Dilalu is still in the city."

"He was near the docks. The merchant could have sailed to Cyprus by now."

Kysen opened his eyes and sat up with a grimace. "Tcha said he was scurrying down an alley away from the docks."

Meren dropped the rush pen he'd been using, leaned forward in his chair and said, "The docks."

Kysen met his gaze. "Abu went with the men who searched that area. If Bener were there, he would have found her. You know that, Father."

"Yes, but . . ." Meren shook his head and sat back. "You're right. And I dare not go myself, although—"

"You'd feel better if you could tear every warehouse and shed apart with your own hands," Kysen said.

Meren nodded.

"I have been out there searching, Father. All it does is make me feel useless and powerless."

"But at least you were doing something."

They spent a few more hours going over everything they'd found out in their investigations. By the time they finished Meren was in a peculiar state of agitation and exhaustion. Kysen studied him covertly, as if he expected his father to collapse. When Meren ordered Kysen to get some rest, he wouldn't go until Meren also promised to shut his eyes. So as early morning approached Meren bathed and lay down. The house was silent except for the hollow deep-toned croaking of the frogs in the reflection pools.

Usually this rhythmic serenade lulled him to sleep, but his eyes were open in the darkness long after Zar had extinguished the alabaster lamps and retired. That irksome feeling of having forgotten something had returned. His chest burned, and no matter how many times he went over every piece of information, he couldn't identify anything that might be the source of this nagging sensation. If only he could figure out what he'd overlooked or forgotten, he might discover the identity of the murderer.

But what good would it do now? Knowing who the evil one was wouldn't save Bener. All he could do was wait, and wait, and wait. He groaned and sat up. Donning a kilt, he padded out of his rooms, across the reception hall, and across the front courtyard. There Abu stood talking to the men he'd posted at the front gate.

"Lord," the charioteer said. "You should be resting."

"I can't." He wondered if Abu could read in his voice the panic that threatened to engulf him.

"There is no word of her, lord. At least lie down. I will come to you the moment I know anything."

"Don't tell me to rest," Meren snapped.

He flung himself away from the group by the gate and strode toward one of the reflection pools that lay between the perimeter wall and the house. If he didn't master himself, he would do something reckless or worse, go mad.

"Lord Meren!"

Meren turned to find Irzanen rushing through the gate, and after him, holding his hand, stumbled a slight figure.

Without a word Meren raced toward them, his heart pounding. He lunged, caught Bener in his arms, and squeezed her so hard she let out a squeak of protest. He babbled at her, demanding to know if she was well, what had happened to her, why she didn't cry out, and a thousand other fervid questions. After a long while he calmed enough to be able to put her down, but kept hold of her. She was trembling and crying silently.

"Did they hurt you?" he asked again with a fierce, rough tone.

"No, Father."

"Are you certain?"

Through her tears Bener said, "I ought to know whether I'm hurt or not, Father."

If she could make such a retort, she was well. The relief that flooded his body nearly turned his legs to water. His throat knotted, and he could do nothing but stand there and hold Bener.

Abu appeared, grinning. "I posted men on the streets around the house to watch for her."

"She just appeared around a corner," Irzanen said, hovering near Bener. "There was no one with her."

Bener's voice shook. "They took me to the square near the temple of Ptah and set me free, so I came home."

Meren silently thanked all the gods at once, then spoke to the jubilant Irzanen. "Go to Lord Kysen and tell him his sister has been released."

Holding Bener at arm's length, he examined her from head to foot before speaking again. "Who took you?"

"May the gods damn him to oblivion," Bener said as she wiped her eyes on the hem of her gown.

"Who was it?"

"I don't know! I was mad at Irzanen and wanted to walk awhile before I returned to the guests, so I went down the path to the garden, and he grabbed me. He was hiding in the shadows beside one of the incense trees."

"Did his voice sound familiar? Was he a big man? Did you see or hear anything while he held you?"

"Father, please." Bener threw up her hands. "He dropped a foul-smelling sack over my head and held a knife to my side. I had no chance to see anything then or later. Afterward they kept me in a room with shuttered windows. Most of the time I was bound, gagged, and blindfolded." She bit her lip and sobbed. "I couldn't see, I couldn't see anything, and I thought they were going to kill me. He told me to give you a message." Her voice rose, quivering. "He said—tell Lord Meren that my reach is as long as the Nile, my vision like the falcon and the owl, my power greater than pharaoh's. I could reach her if you sealed her in the mightiest pyramid."

She sobbed again. Meren cursed and picked her up. Holding his weeping daughter, he shouted over his shoulder. "Abu, send for the physician."

Chapter 14

Kysen had seldom seen his father in a rage. The Eyes and Ears of Pharaoh was known for his brilliance, for his mastery of intrigue and diplomacy, but above all for his precise self-control. For years Kysen had tried to emulate his father's discipline, and he marveled now that Meren could restrain his fury at Bener in order to question her about her abductors.

The sun was up by the time the physician Nebamun had examined her. She had washed and eaten, and now she was resting on a couch beneath an arbor in the garden. Anath had joined them, and she and Kysen were watching Meren guide his daughter through another description of her ordeal. His gentle queries were designed to prod her memory, but there was little to be gained.

"Take time to think," Meren said. "You heard nothing unusual while you were being held? No other voices, no animals, no children, no sounds like someone grinding grain or paddling through water?"

"I'm sorry, Father. I suppose there was no unsealed window or vent in the room." Bener's eyes were red from weeping, but she was calmer. She looked tired and unhappy.

"And you're certain you've never previously heard the voices of the ones who held you."

"Yes, I'm certain, but there were three of them, I think."

"Were they voices of young men or old ones?"

"Neither." Bener sighed. "They could have had twenty years or forty." She brightened and sat up on the couch. "But they weren't noblemen."

Meren approached her and asked, "How do you know?"

"They spoke more like Kysen did when he first joined the family," Bener said.

Kysen said, "That's hardly surprising. There are far more commoners than nobles."

"But it does mean they weren't foreigners," Anath said, "which eliminates Dilalu and Zulaya, who employ Asiatics for the most part." She sat down beside Bener and hugged her. "I was so worried about you."

Bener rested her head on Anath's shoulder. "I thought they were going to kill me."

Kysen watched Meren as he walked away, his arms folded over his chest, his head down. Meren strolled among the flower beds for a while, and then slowly walked back to the group under the arbor.

"You should get some rest, Bener," he said. "But before you go I give you this command. You are never again to involve yourself in my work."

Bener jumped to her feet. "But, Father, it's not my fault that I was taken."

"Perhaps not, but had you remained within your proper sphere, the idea of abducting you might not have occurred to the murderer."

"But—"

"Silence!"

Meren's roar made Kysen jump. Anath gave a start and scowled at Meren. Bener skittered backward and would have stumbled had Kysen not steadied her. Meren's glittering gaze fixed on his daughter, and Kysen was suddenly glad he hadn't been the one abducted.

"I have spoken, and there will be an end to your defiance," Meren said, his voice vibrating with suppressed anger. "And to ensure your compliance I'm assigning a bodyguard to watch you."

"Father, no," Bener said, her eyes filling with tears.

"Now, Meren," Anath said, rising from the couch. "I know you've been badly frightened and that your fear prompts you to do this, but you must see that Bener wasn't at fault."

"Stay out of this," Meren snapped.

Anath's eyes narrowed, and Kysen held his breath. The Eyes of Babylon didn't tolerate dismissal well, but to his surprise she seemed to relent. Her gaze softened. Indeed her whole body seemed to soften. Her voice lowered and took on a sensual quality Kysen had never heard.

"Meren, my love, please," Anath said.

She approached his father with a hip-swinging walk that astounded Kysen. He watched the golden girdle on her hips sway, noted the way the long strands of gold and turquoise beads that hung from it swished between her legs. She stopped beside his father, regarded him with her hands clasped behind her back and her head tilted up to meet his gaze.

Meren barely looked at her, and Kysen could see that he'd grown wary.

"What?"

"If you're determined to have your poor daughter watched,

allow me to do it. Better a woman than one of your hulking charioteers."

Meren's mouth had settled into a straight line, a sign of determination, but Kysen watched the line slowly curve. It wasn't a smile, but it was close.

Kysen glanced at Bener, who gave him a pleading look. He said, "It's a good idea, Father. Anath can watch her more closely than a man could."

"You give your word she won't escape your attention?" Meren asked.

"Of course," Anath said. "I'll stay here for a few days. She needs someone right now."

Meren brooded silently, then nodded. "Very well."

"Good," Anath said. "Come, Bener. We'll go to your room. I have a potion from a wise woman of Babylon that will help you get some sleep."

As the two women left Kysen went to stand beside Meren. "Father, what was that all about?"

"What?" Meren asked as he watched the women.

"Meren, my love? I've never heard a woman address you like that."

"I am happy to have provided you with a new experience," Meren said.

Kysen waited, but Meren said nothing further. It was useless to ask any questions. When his father decided to be circumspect, only a royal command could make him reveal anything. Something had happened between Anath and Meren on the journey to Syene. There was a subtle intimacy in the way they talked to each other, an almost tangible and equally intimate tension between them. Kysen raised his brows and gave his father a sideways glance, but Meren refused to meet his eyes.

There had been other women, of course, but Meren had

never allowed any of them to behave toward him as Anath had. An unspoken assumption lay between the two that each had a certain right to the other. It was this understanding that was the source of Kysen's amazement and which convinced him, as he left his father in the garden, that Meren and Anath were more than lovers.

The waning of the day saw Kysen in his guise as Nen enter the house of Othrys. Othrys had saved Meren's life not long ago, and he was privy to their search for Nefertiti's killer. The pirate lived in a labyrinthine dwelling of Greek design with a hall dominated by circular central hearth and a clerestory window high above it. Two muscle-burdened guards became his intimate friends the moment he appeared, watching his every movement, preventing him from straying. A steward guided him through the maze of rooms and corridors, on to a loggia and into a garden. Soft, haunting music was coming from somewhere, and the farther they went into the garden the closer they came to the source.

Finally Kysen spotted the place from which the notes issued. In the midst of a stand of trees sat a small pavilion unlike anything Kysen had seen. It was constructed of creamy limestone, but the lintel over the door was of white marble carved with spirals. Two slim, engaged half columns flanked the portal. Of green marble, they had been carved with alternating bands of spirals and hatched chevrons.

Kysen had never realized just how wealthy piracy had made Othrys. To have imported marble of such high quality and install it in a house rather than a temple or tomb, such extravagance on the part of a commoner was unheard of. Kysen walked up the front steps after the steward and closely followed by his silent, weapon-laden friends. As he crossed the threshold a young woman passed him. Kysen glimpsed lapis lazuli eyes and long waves of hair the color of red gold.

She hardly glanced his way, but Kysen saw her long enough to notice several things. She wore a fortune in gold and blue enamel jewelry—a necklace of bracelets the beads of which had been shaped in the form of rosettes and spirals, and all covered in minute granulation. She wore a costly embroidered gown of sea green secured with gold and silver pins, and she bore a great resemblance to Othrys. Kysen dragged his gaze away from her when one of his guards glared and shoved him.

Othrys was sitting in a chair playing a harp. The steward spoke briefly to his master and left. The guards followed him, but they stopped just outside the door and stood watching Kysen. Othrys took no notice of his guest and continued to play. The pirate was a well-built man near Meren's age, but unlike Meren the hillocks and knolls of his muscles were crisscrossed with scars, white slashes against the light brown of his skin. Like Meren his body was hardened from physical exercise and the exertions of battle, but in place of a dark, concealing gaze were eyes of the glaring white-blue of the sky at midday. He was wearing a blue tunic and gold belt, leggings and sandals.

Othrys seemed in no rush to speak to Kysen. He plucked a last note on the harp and gazed out of the wide, open windows of the pavilion. They were as tall as a man and five times as wide, allowing the outside to come in along with the breeze. Finally the pirate sighed and turned to Kysen.

"So, your father didn't die."

"He sends his thanks and begs to be allowed to show his gratitude for your help in his time of desperation," Kysen said.

Othrys smiled and set the harp aside. "Spoken with true Egyptian courtliness and breeding, but I'm certain I'll have occasion to ask Lord Meren to repay his debt to me."

Kysen refrained from commenting. He could imagine many favors Othrys might need from his father, but few Meren would be willing to grant. Othrys rose and went to a long table where he poured wine into two fluted stone goblets and handed one to Kysen.

"May the good will of the Earth Mother bless you, friend Kysen. It's late in the day for business."

"The business of the Eyes and Ears of Pharaoh knows no late hour," Kysen replied.

"Ah, you mean the days of pharaoh's agents are long. I assume you've come about Dilalu," Othrys said. "I got your message and sent men in search of him, but learned nothing. He's hiding somewhere, and his people are silent about him, which is odd. Usually I can bribe someone to talk."

"He's frightened. We came to blows at the Divine Lotus." Kysen frowned. "He'd been warned by someone that he was in danger, because he had mercenaries concealed somewhere in the tavern. They even tried to take me prisoner."

"How could Dilalu know you were going to be at the Divine Lotus?" Othrys asked as he sat down again and turned his face to the breeze. "It's more likely that he's cheated someone in a trade and must protect himself from the wrath of his victim."

"Perhaps. A dealer in weapons and mercenaries makes enemies easily." Kysen set his goblet down. "I must go."

Othrys glanced at him. "I heard you met Zulaya and have become well acquainted with him."

"More gossip from Mistress Ese?"

"Many people find it wise to make themselves familiar with those to whom Zulaya grants his friendship. The event is so rare." Othrys lifted his face to the breeze again, closed his eyes, and said softly, "Beware."

"I fail to see the sense in your wariness of Zulaya," Kysen said. "Neither my father nor I have discovered anything about him that would mark him as more dangerous than any of a dozen such men. Besides, he wasn't even in Egypt until after—" He glanced back at the guards and lowered his voice. "He didn't come to Egypt until after the queen was murdered."

Othrys set his wine down and picked up a round ivory spice box carved with winged griffins. He shook a bit of powderlike spice from it into his goblet and swirled the liquid.

"I'm not surprised. That's the way he conducts business, at a distance, so that nothing can be traced to him. He might not have been in Horizon of the Aten, but his agents could have done his bidding. There were hundreds of foreigners there. Merchants came in with the trading ships endlessly. And there were the foreign delegations to the court, emissaries from other rulers, retinues of the vassal princes, all trekking out to those cursed desert altars and parading at Akhenaten's jubilees and celebrations of the Aten."

Suddenly alert, Kysen said, "You were there?"

"Yes, of course."

"You never told me."

Othrys shrugged. "It didn't seem important."

Kysen barely heard him. This was one of those times when his view of things changed abruptly and drastically. He'd always assumed Othrys had been in Memphis or the Greek city-state of Mycenae or on one of his pirating expeditions at sea. Othrys was toying with the lid to the ivory box. Kysen walked back to Othrys, studying him closely.

"How long were you there?"

"How should I know? I was there off and on many times over the years until the court moved back to Memphis and Thebes."

"When the queen was killed?"

The pirate's hands stilled with the lid to the ivory spice box in them. "Aye, by the Earth Mother. I was there when she was poisoned, my friend. And if you value your pretty head you'd better not ask me if I killed the queen."

Kysen heard a menacing note in the pirate's voice and cursed to himself. He'd made a dangerous blunder, one any novice could have avoided. So he smiled his father's ingenuous and deceiving smile.

"Be at ease, Othrys. Had I any suspicions of you, I would never have asked such a question. At least not here, not without a company of royal archers and a squadron of charioteers behind me."

Othrys left off his executioner's stare and laughed. "Forgive me. In my trade one doesn't survive without an overabundance of suspicion."

"As one whose task it is to be suspicious of all, I readily forgive," Kysen said with a bow. "And I must give you my thanks and go. I must meet with a mutual acquaintance, Tcha."

"You're welcome to him, my friend. I'd sooner face a thousand sea demons than come near that walking garbage pit."

Kysen left the pirate's house in a state of agitation. Reia was waiting for him outside, and Kysen told the charioteer about his discovery as they walked through the streets of the Caverns.

Soon they both fell silent. Othrys had been at Horizon of the Aten all along and hadn't mentioned the fact. Why? Had his information about Dilalu, Yamen, and Zulaya been false, a ruse to distract attention from himself? Kysen began to look around as they moved through alleys and streets, but he detected no sign that they'd been followed. As they neared the appointed meeting place, his wariness faded. Had Othrys's slip been incriminating, he'd have sent men to deal with Kysen and Reia immediately. Or would he?

Deep in thought, Kysen reached the meeting place, a refuse heap behind a warehouse in the Caverns. He leaned against a wall and studied the cracks that marred its plaster surface. He wasn't going to solve this new mystery right away, and if he didn't pay attention to what he was doing he could get into trouble. Ugly things happened to those foolish enough to become distracted in the Caverns.

A slave trudged out of a house across the street and hurled the contents of a scrap pot onto the festering pile. Waves of transparent heat floated from its surface along with a sickly sweet odor that had driven Kysen to take his position upwind. He'd been watching this noxious mountain for a good reason. The thief and informant called Tcha made a habit of checking waste mounds for castoffs that might be worth something, and they'd arranged a meeting.

His father was still at home conspicuously doing nothing other than routine business, which was why Kysen was prowling again. He had to find Dilalu, and Tcha had been asking about the merchant among his low but numerous acquaintances. Kysen straightened as a scrawny little figure with greasy hair and more scars than skin shuffled into view. Tcha skulked around the refuse heap, acquiring a cloak of flies as he went, and joined Kysen. He scuttled into a shadow, darting uneasy glances around the area.

"No one's here, Tcha. Reia is down that alley watching, and that's the only way in."

"Didn't see no charioteer, master."

"You weren't supposed to see him. Now what have you learned?"

"It be hard work, finding things out, master. I've trudged from one end of the city to the other." Tcha pointed to Kysen's feet. "Never had no fine leather sandals to protect my feet. Never had no protector to watch out for me. Life is hard, master."

"You're not getting more than I agreed to pay, so quit complaining," Kysen said.

Tcha opened his mouth, but a rattling cough issued from his throat. He put the whole force of his lungs behind the cough, bent over and groaned, then leaned weakly against the wall.

"The wind blew a terrible amount of dust into me, master. I'm sure it blew a desert fiend in too, and it cursed me and that's why I got this rattle in my chest. Got nothing to pay a magician or doctor. Just going to waste away, me."

Kysen lifted an eyebrow, but said nothing. Tcha sank against the wall with dramatic effect, and gave a high-pitched moan. Kysen's foot swept around and knocked the thief's legs from under him. Tcha hit the ground with a screech, but Kysen grabbed a handful of sticky hair and hauled him to his feet, shaking him with each word.

"Tell me what you've found out." He released Tcha.

"Ow! Broke my neck, I'm certain of it." When Kysen moved toward him again he backed away. "All right, all right, master. I heard of a man who might know where the merchant's got to." Tcha rubbed his neck and put some distance between himself and Kysen. "He used to work for Dilalu as a trader's assistant, but he was dismissed because he drank too much."

"Where is he?" Kysen asked.

"Probably at a place called the Heart Scarab. It's near that old wrecked shrine to the god Shu. He goes there because the beer is cheaper than at the Divine Lotus."

Kysen eyed the thief, who had suddenly become more fidgety than usual. "What's wrong with you?"

"Naught, master."

Kysen studied Tcha, but decided the little man simply wasn't used to anyone taking notice of him for any length of time. "Does this drunkard have a name?"

"O' course, master. Name's Marduk something. Impossible to say these foreign names. He's known as Marduk."

"Well done," Kysen said as he rubbed the palm that had touched Tcha's hair against his kilt. It felt sticky.

He handed the thief several bronze beads on a string, leftovers from a necklace his sister Isis had broken. Tcha's eyes grew big, and he clutched the beads to his chest.

"Thank you, master." He bobbed up and down in gratitude.

Tcha had expected to be cheated, Kysen was sure. It was a realistic expectation given the people with whom he usually consorted. Still clutching his treasure, Tcha began to sneak away, but he hesitated. Casting wary glances all around, he sidled up to Kysen, wet his lips, and spoke in a voice so low Kysen had to bend down to hear it.

"You be careful at the Heart Scarab, master."

"Why?"

Tcha's glance slid away, and he muttered, "Always should take care around here." He shuffled off, talking to himself. "Never had no beads like these before. Never had no jewels, nor good sandals, nor nice, soft kilt. Never. Never, never, never."

Chapter 15

Kysen eyed Tcha's stunted figure and contemplated calling him back to demand the significance of his last warning, but then he shook his head. He just wasn't used to Tcha's gratitude, and there wasn't much time. He didn't want to remain in the Caverns too long. There was always the chance that someone in the employ of Nefertiti's murderer might see him and recognize Lord Kysen, the son of Meren. Kysen walked back down the alley to where Reia waited and headed for the ruined shrine of the god Shu.

The Heart Scarab turned out to be a gathering hole for the dregs of the city—derelict servants, leather workers smelling of curing salts and urine, street thieves, embalmer's assistants, and drunks. The place was named for the beetle-shaped amulet placed in the wrappings of a mummy in order to prevent the deceased's heart from testifying against him in the netherworld. If the heart revealed evil deeds during the soul's judgment, the dead person was cast into oblivion. An apt name considering the patrons of the place.

With Reia behind him, Kysen walked across a packed-earth floor littered with food scraps and spilt, sour beer. Inert bodies lay in poses of destitution and stupor from one end of the tavern's single room to the other. The proprietor had pointed out a slumped, fleshy man in a corner when Kysen inquired after Marduk.

Standing over the man, Kysen noted his curling beard, the ringlets in his hair, his dirty nails, and soiled wool robe. He was dozing on a stool with a beer jar clutched in both hands.

"Marduk?"

There wasn't a response. He exchanged glances with Reia, who was watching the rest of the tavern's patrons.

"Marduk," Kysen repeated. When the man didn't stir, he nudged him with his toe. The man snorted and came awake.

"Wha—"

"You are the Asiatic called Marduk?"

"Go away." Marduk turned his shoulder and snuggled into his corner.

Kysen pulled the stool from under Marduk, and the Asiatic hit the floor hard.

"Aargh! May Baal curse your children's children. What do you want, Egyptian?"

"It is said you might know the whereabouts of a certain Asiatic called Dilalu."

Marduk scowled at Kysen. "Who be you to ask me anything?"

Kysen knelt beside the man and produced a bronze ring with a turquoise bezel. "I'm the man who's willing to pay to be able to ask you anything."

Marduk's scowl vanished. He laughed so loud Kysen winced, and he clapped his benefactor on the back.

"Help me up, my friend. Come share a jar of beer. I have two. Where's that other one?" Marduk snatched a jar that stood on the floor near his corner and thrust it into Kysen's hands. He waved his own jar so that the beer sloshed out, and laughed again. "Let us drink in honor of friendship."

"I don't want a drink."

Marduk's joviality disappeared instantly. "You don't want to drink with me? Why not? Marduk is good enough to drink with fine lords and great men. I don't answer the questions of men who refuse a friendly jar of beer."

Casting a rueful glance at Reia, Kysen took the cup Marduk offered and poured beer through the straining holes in the jar. He took a sip and grimaced at the acrid taste. The stuff was poorly made and flavored with some cheap spice that failed to hide the flatness of the brew. Marduk must have thought it as fine as Syrian wine, however, for he insisted that Kysen drink most of the jar before he began answering questions.

"That old cheat Dilalu? He cast me off near a week ago. I heard he'd gone into hiding. Only Baal knows why. He's wealthy enough to buy his way out of trouble."

"Do you know where he might be found?" Kysen asked as he took another painful sip of beer.

Marduk drained his cup, slapped it down on the table, and pretended to consider carefully, his eyes raised to the ceiling in thought. "Well, young one, as I remember, when Dilalu ran into evil-wishers he didn't trust to leave him be, he went to ground at his harlot's place."

"Where is that?"

"The dwelling of Mistress Henut, third house from the corner in the Street of the Locusts, beside the sandal maker's house."

"I'm unfamiliar with this Street of the Locusts," Kysen said. The beer was causing a faint buzzing noise in his head. "If you'll take me there, I'll stand the cost of two jars of beer."

"Five jars."

"Three," Kysen said.

Marduk slapped his thigh. "Done! Let us hurry, my friend, so that we may start drinking those jars all the sooner."

Kysen followed Marduk outside to find that dusk was rapidly turning to night. That buzzing sound seemed to be louder outside, and his eyes were beginning to hurt. With difficulty he tracked Marduk's progress through the crooked streets, dodging street vendors, donkeys, women with water jars or baskets on their heads. Once he glanced over his shoulder to see Reia loping steadily after him, but he had to hurry to catch up with Marduk.

He shoved his way through a crowd around a baker selling fresh loaves to find Marduk was far ahead of him. He worked his way through the crowds headed away from one of the city's many markets, but each step became more difficult, as if stone weights had been tied to his ankles. His chest heaved with the effort to catch his breath, and the fading day seemed as hot as the hour when Ra reached his highest point.

Finally he saw Marduk ahead. He shoved a young woman aside, almost ran into the stall of a cloth vendor, and stopped. His mouth dry, he shouted for Marduk to wait. The man turned and stared at him. Why was he staring? Kysen blinked sweat out of his eyes as he met Marduk's gaze. Suddenly the Asiatic dashed into the crowd. Kysen tried to run after him, but he couldn't lift his legs. He concentrated hard, in spite of the heat, the sweat, the pressing crowd.

Someone was shouting at him. He turned to find Reia approaching, but the charioteer seemed to be running with a strangely slow gait, as if he were wading. Kysen finally got one foot to move. He took a step toward Reia and laughed.

Reia broke through the thick air Kysen had been fighting
and came up to him.

"Lord!"

Kysen laughed again, but the market seemed to tilt and
spin, and he clutched a post of one of the vendor stalls.
Reia said his name again. Now everything he heard seemed
muted the way one perceived sounds when underwater.

"Marduk ran away," Kysen said.

This was the most amusing thing that had ever happened
to him, so he laughed again, only this time he couldn't stop.
He laughed until his stomach hurt.

"Lord, you must come with me at once," Reia said, grabbing Kysen.

Kysen snatched his arm free. "I can walk. Watch me."

He took a step, and his bones turned to water. He hurtled toward the ground, but Reia caught him. Kysen flung
his arm over the charioteer's shoulder.

"I think you'd better take me home." He looked into Reia's
fear-filled eyes and smiled. "I can't seem to keep my eyes
open. Funny, I didn't think I drank that much."

With a soft chuckle Kysen leaned heavily against Reia. As
darkness enveloped him he grinned. At least his legs didn't
feel like granite anymore.

Meren strode around the reception hall dictating orders
and letters, business long neglected during his disgrace and
illness. Bener had accompanied Anath home to gather a few
belongings for her stay at Golden House. With great effort
he concentrated on reports from vassal cities like Joppa,
Megiddo, Jericho, and Hazor, trying to sift through rumor
and fact. Close scrutiny was essential in these tumultuous
times in order to catch the first hint of conspiracy before
it led to open rebellion.

Because of Akhenaten's neglect, some of the petty princes had forgotten how far pharaoh's arm might stretch in defense of his caravans and military outposts. The key to Tutankhamun's policy was to maintain the empire without having to intervene with troops unless absolutely necessary. This meant using alternatives to the military, one of which was gathering intelligence and using it against the king's enemies. Even more worrying was the threat the Hittites posed to the northernmost regions of the empire.

Meren read a dispatch and sighed. "Answer to the captain of the garrison at Tyre. I have received your report and will intercede on your behalf with General Nakhtmin. Until the rations due your men can be delivered I authorize you to purchase bolts of cloth and other necessary provisions." He glanced at Bek, who was sitting cross-legged on the floor and writing. "Remind me to send a message to the general so that he can send linen on the next supply ship, and write to the nearest agent. Have him investigate the supply situation at Tyre. Something is wrong, and I'm willing to wager that someone's diverting ration goods before they're unloaded at the dock. Also make inquiries at the delta port where the ships are loaded."

Sometimes minor snarls indicated a larger problem, one involving the corruption of royal officials. Meren hoped this wasn't the case, because he was growing weary of chastising wrongdoers. Many of his friends felt the same way—Maya, Horemheb, Ay. His old mentor had seen much in his life, including the long reign of Amunhotep the Magnificent, and that of his successor, Akhenaten. Corruption was an ever-present threat, a disease that had to be exorcised lest it rot the kingdom from within. Sometimes Meren felt he was fighting a war for harmony and balance while almost everyone else seemed undisturbed by chaos and perversion.

He dropped the dispatch on a pile near the master's dais. A high, loud wail rolled toward him from somewhere inside the house. It was Remi, Kysen's little son, protesting some correction from his nurse, but the sound penetrated Meren's body like a spear. The cry reminded him of the sounds of grief made by mourners at a funeral, Nefertiti's funeral, when Tutankhamun was little more than a babe and had been called Tutankhaten.

The day they entombed the queen had been as bright and cloudless as any other. Dust blew across the sun-blasted plain in which Horizon of the Aten lay, but the funeral procession was not what Nefertiti would have chosen. Instead of a journey by funeral boat across the river to a tomb in the west, the land of the dead, her magnificent coffin was being taken east, in the direction of the rising sun.

As he trudged along behind the royal family in their golden chariots, Meren heard again the long eerie moan, the sound of thousands of voices raised in grief for their queen. Stylized, slow of rhythm, it rose from the city and sailed upward, carried on the air to rebound off the cliffs as if the ghosts that inhabited the desert had risen to welcome another soul. An answering wail came from the princesses and their attendants, but Akhenaten, resplendent in his chariot, remained silent. This was his first public appearance since the death of the great royal wife.

The journey to the royal tomb was long, and the route took the funeral cortege up the gradual rise of barren ground behind Horizon of the Aten and into the cliffs that marked the high eastern desert. The solar orb glared its light and heat directly above the mourners by the time the queen's coffin arrived at the entrance to its new abode. Meren had to squint in order to watch the priests maneuver the funeral sledge toward the mouth of the

tomb. As befitted a queen and pharaoh, Nefertiti had been encased in gold and precious jewels.

Not long ago he remembered her saying, "Meren, I would
trade all I possess, down to the tiniest jewel, for the return of
just one of my daughters from the netherworld." Now she was
going to join them.

At the tomb entrance Akhenaten was performing ceremonies
to ensure his wife's rebirth. He chanted a prayer detailing her
journey to join the Aten. Nefertiti would have wanted the traditional rites so that she could make the perilous journey through
the netherworld to the Hall of Judgment. But the old ways were
not permitted, the old gods ignored. Meren only hoped the old
ones would see the queen's true heart and save her ka before
Akhenaten's heresy destroyed her soul.

He heard a child crying. Little Tutankhaten was frightened,
and Meren could see his nurse trying to quiet the child. Ay motioned to him, and Meren swiftly walked over and picked the
boy up. Tutankhaten protested, but Meren put his hand on the
back of the child's head and guided it to his shoulder. The boy
snuffled into his neck for a moment, and then subsided. Ay nodded his gratitude as another wailing refrain issued from the
princesses.

As Meren watched, Ay closed his eyes and bowed his head.
Then Akhenaten finished his prayer, and to Meren's astonishment he barked at the women. The mourners' cries went silent,
and the king raised his voice in praise of the Aten. Meren kept
his expression carefully reverent. On his shoulder Tutankhamun
slept. He gave the boy back to his nurse.

Just then Ay lifted his bowed head. Meren had expected to
see grief; he hadn't expected rage that contained within it the hor-
rors of the netherworld. Ay tore his gaze from the golden prison
to which Nefertiti's body had been consigned. It rose and settled
on Akhenaten, and the pain and rage magnified. His creased face

seemed to fold in on itself, and he staggered against the side of the tomb entrance. Smenkhare, Akhenaten's brother and heir, supported Ay as Meren moved swiftly to his aid. The prince left Ay in Meren's care as the ceremonial procession headed inside the tomb and down the long, rock-hewn corridor to the burial chamber.

The last of the mourners vanished inside before Ay could stand. He leaned on Meren, took a step, and stopped to mutter under his breath. "I killed her."

"What?"

"As surely as if I had driven a dagger into her heart."

Meren shook his head. "It wasn't your fault she became ill."

Ay paused before the first step down the long ramp that led to the burial chamber and met Meren's eyes. In spite of the dim light his gaze shone with a radiance born of near madness.

"Be silent, my son," he hissed. "I could have prevented all of this. And now I curse the day I agreed to wed my daughter to the son of pharaoh. Nefertiti died because of my ambition." Ay's voice rose. "I am responsible, and the gods will rightly punish me for my sin!"

Meren roused from his memories when Anath and Bener entered the hall followed by servants bearing chests and baskets. Anath gave him a smile as she sailed by him on her way to a guest chamber. Bener gave directions to the servants, her brow furrowed with some lingering distress. Meren watched her, noting the way she clasped her hands tightly, how her stance had become rigid, her eyes sorrowful. She'd been far more cheerful before she left with Anath, but now her fear had returned. Bouts of distress would no doubt occur, which worried Meren and made him feel powerless, which in turn fed his fury at the evil one responsible.

Bener finished giving instructions and came to him. "Father, I want to talk to you."

"You're not going to change my decision," he said. "You're going to be watched for your own good."

"I know, but—Kysen!"

Meren turned to see Reia and Abu carrying Kysen's limp body. Meren rushed to them as they lowered him to the floor.

"He's unconscious, lord," Reia said before Meren could speak. "We went to a tavern called the Heart Scarab and met a man called Marduk, who had been a servant of Dilalu. Lord Kysen drank with him to discover the whereabouts of the merchant. Marduk was leading us to him when Kysen fell ill."

A feeling of unreality settled over Meren as he searched Kysen's face for signs of life. This couldn't be happening. He couldn't face another threat to a beloved child.

"I've sent for the physician," Abu added.

Meren touched Kysen's neck with the tips of his fingers, searching for the voice of the heart. He felt it, quick, but faint. Without a word he picked up his son and strode out of the hall. He reached Kysen's bed, lay his son down, and whirled around to snarl at Abu.

"Where is Nebamun?"

"I've sent for him, lord. He's on his way."

Bener hurried in with a bowl of water and a cloth. She began weeping as she bathed Kysen's brow, and Meren swallowed hard as he watched his two children.

So recently banished, the horrific feeling of impotence crushed his heart. Ignoring it, he snapped at Abu. "Take men and find this Marduk. Bring him to me. Don't come back without him."

"Aye, lord."

Abu left, but returned at once holding a folded and sealed note, his expression grave. "Another message, lord. Given by a little boy paid to deliver it."

Meren stared at the blank seal, then broke it and read.

Now you endure the punishment for disobedience. My hand is around his heart. If I desire it, he dies.

The papyrus dropped from Meren's stiff fingers. Dazed, he neither spoke nor moved when Bener picked up the message.

"Oh," she gasped. Tears streamed over her face, and she took Kysen's hand in both of hers.

From deep in her chest rose a long, keening wail, and for the second time that day Meren was back in a desert tomb, pierced by the mourner's cry.

Chapter 16

Meren stood beside Kysen's bed listening to his physician. Abu had gone in search of the one called Marduk, still hampered by the need for secrecy. Meren had debated the risk, considering that his earlier efforts at secrecy had failed, but desperation overruled caution.

Bener still sat near her brother and held his hand. Kysen remained in a deathlike state, his face paler than desert sand, the voice of his heart faint. Meren watched Kysen's chest rise slowly, then fall. Each pause between movements caused him agony.

Without taking his gaze from the shallow movement he said, "So you don't know what's wrong?"

"He has been given a poison of some kind, lord. Not poison of the tekau plant, but there are many herbs that could produce this state. Unless I'm certain of the cause, treating him might do harm. If he were awake I would make him vomit to rid his body of the evil it swallowed. For now, it is safer to watch and wait. He's strong; his ka will fight the poison if I perform certain rites in his aid."

"Do so at once," Meren said.

As Nebamun busied himself with the contents of his physician's box Reia came in and saluted.

"You sent for me, lord?"

With a last look at Kysen, Meren moved away from the bed. "Tell me what happened from the moment you left this house."

The charioteer related the day's events, and Meren stopped him after he told of the visit to Othrys.

"He saw the pirate alone?"

"He said it's difficult to see Othrys at all, and having a charioteer at his side would make it impossible."

"He's right," Meren said. "But he told you he had wine with Othrys."

"Yes, lord, but he didn't become ill until after drinking with that Asiatic."

"What else did he say?"

Reia glanced at Kysen's prone body, and a spasm of remorse passed across his face. "When he left the pirate's house he was agitated. He said he'd discovered that Othrys had been at Horizon of the Aten when the queen died. He said that—"

Meren cursed. "You're certain?"

"Yes, lord. He was disturbed, and said if we didn't find Dilalu soon we would return and tell you about it."

A wave of chill dread passed over Meren, and the panic he'd fought against so long raged unchecked. "Damn you, Reia, if Othrys has been lying all along, and Kysen found out—"

"The pirate," Reia said.

Their eyes met, and they both sprang for the door. Meren got there first and flung it open. He ran through Golden House with Reia at his heels, his heart burning with thoughtless rage. He burst onto the loggia and came to a sudden halt. Reia nearly ran into him. He stood still, distracted and uncertain. The pirate had never entered into his evaluation of the queen's murder, and Othrys knew too much. If he was guilty, he posed a lethal threat. Reia was watching him anxiously.

"I can't take the chance," Meren muttered. He glanced at Reia. "But I can't rush to attack and risk him dying before I force him to tell me what he's done to Kysen." He ran his hand through his hair. "We'll do this another way."

Hurrying to his office, Meren penned a courteous note requesting a visit from Othrys. Reia left to give it to a porter. When he returned Meren gave him quiet instructions and returned to Kysen's bedside to watch Nebamun cast spells of protection and healing. It was dark by the time Othrys arrived.

Meren received the pirate on the master's dais in the hall. Striding in as if he were walking across the deck of one of his ships, Othrys stopped at the steps of the dais, planted his hands on his hips, and gave Meren an annoyed scowl.

"Greetings, Egyptian. What news have you that I must leave my table and my guests and rush across the city to hear it?"

Meren made a concise motion with his hand, and chari-oteers appeared at every door to the hall. Othrys looked at them and narrowed his eyes.

"What game is this?"

Leaning forward in his chair, Meren spoke softly with a calm he didn't feel. "My son has been poisoned. He lies near death, and if you are responsible, I will have the remedy from you or by all the gods I'll tear your heart out with my bare hands. You have until the count of ten to confess." Meren sat back. "One."

The charioteers began to close in on Othrys. His gaze darted from one group to the other.

"Two."

"You're mad," he snarled.

"Three." The charioteers surrounded Othrys.

"Four."

"I did nothing!"

"You failed to reveal your presence at Horizon of the Aten when the queen died. Five."

"It wasn't important," Othrys cried as the charioteers grabbed his arms and legs.

"Six." Meren stood. "Every scrap of information you gave to me could have been designed to lead me away from you. Seven."

"If I was who you say, I could have killed you when you came to me for help, you fool."

"You might have intended to kill me and were prevented," Meren said as he came down the dais steps. "Eight." He drew his dagger.

Othrys was sweating as he strained against the men who held him. "I could have killed you the moment you stepped into my house, by the Earth Mother."

"Nine." Meren positioned himself in front of the pirate.

Othrys uttered an obscenity and spat on the floor. "You're mad."

"You said that. Ten. I think I'll chop your heart out of your chest in the manner of Eater of Souls." Meren raised his dagger.

"Wait!" Othrys rushed on when Meren paused. "I swear by the Earth Mother I did nothing to Kysen. I was at Horizon of the Aten. I didn't tell you because I didn't want to become involved in the contendings of great ones. It never pays. I did no wrong—toward the great royal wife, that is.

I had no reason. She didn't interfere with my affairs. She didn't even know I existed."

Meren looked into the pirate's sky-colored eyes and read fear, desperation, and anger, but nothing else. He shook his head, suddenly uncertain and too filled with his own dread to risk making a fatal mistake. He felt drained. A moment ago he'd been ready to kill this man, suffused with an ungovernable wrath that burned away all moderation, reason, and control. Othrys's protests had broken through the clamor in his head, the urge to take some action, any action. With the return of reason came the feeling of powerlessness. Meren turned away.

"Hold him in the barracks. Make certain he talks to no one."

Meren headed for Kysen's room, the curses and protests of Othrys ringing in his ears as he was dragged out of the hall. Anath had joined Bener in the sickroom, and Nebamun was busy concocting some magical preparation at a table. Meren stood at the foot of the bed and gazed down at his son, who lay as still as a votive figurine. What would he do if he lost Kysen? He winced at the jagged tearing pain the thought provoked. For over ten years this boy had been a part of his life, ever since the day long ago when he encountered that old brute, Pawero, trying to sell his son in the streets of Thebes. He'd been on his way to a meeting with General Horemheb and passed a market in an open area around a well.

"Healthy young boy here!" Pawero had bawled. "Who needs a strong boy for hard labor?"

He glanced at the two, father and son, surprised that any man would hawk his son like a bolt of linen. He looked more closely and saw a scrawny body, inexpertly cropped and dusty hair, and large, half-moon eyes. His gaze traveled rapidly over the purple, yellow, and green blotches on the child's arms, legs, and back. His lower lip was swollen, and he held himself in that careful, still manner that spoke of bruised or cracked ribs. But what fixed in Meren's memory was the child's haunted look, that sorrowful and doomed expression.

All this he saw in a glance and walked on, his steps growing slower and slower. At the edge of the market he turned to look at the pair again. Pawero was entreating a prospective buyer. He suddenly turned and gave the boy a smack on the head.

"Straighten up, Kysen. Show the man your fine muscles."

Kysen held his thin body more erect, and when his father turned away, gave him a look of contempt and defiance that contained the spirit of a warrior. Meren hesitated, admiration dawning. The child had obviously been mistreated for a long time. He could see old scars beneath the bruises. Yet this boy had somehow managed to preserve his courage, which spoke of a strength of heart beyond anything Meren would have expected. As he drew near the well, Pawero kept chattering to his customer with a servile smile plastered on his face.

Kysen looked on, resigned. When the customer moved away, Pawero trotted after him, but the boy remained where he was. It was then that Meren heard him speak for the first time.

"Why don't you beat him into meeting your price?"

Meren almost smiled. "You don't protest being sold?"

The boy started and whirled around to face him. After a few moments of startled contemplation, he shook his head.

"Tried that, master. Just got hit for it."

"I don't understand," Meren said. "A man's son is his staff of old age."

Kysen regarded him with solemn, dark eyes. "I have two older brothers, master." His gaze faltered. "I'm not needed or . . ."

"Wanted?"

The dust-covered head lowered, and the boy said nothing.

"Here! What are you doing bothering a great one?" Pawero swooped at Kysen and punched him in the stomach.

Something snapped inside Meren. He swept around the well, grabbed Pawero by the hair, and dragged him away from the boy. Howling, the man staggered as Meren released him.

"Oh, shut your muzzle," Meren said. "How much for the boy?" He couldn't believe his mouth had uttered the words.

Pawero stopped whining, and his whole being lit with an almost magical glow as he appeared to calculate Meren's wealth. He studied the gold, turquoise, and carnelian broad collar, the beaded belt and bronze dagger.

"Oh, slaves is expensive, great one, especially a boy. Long years of service ahead for him, you know."

Meren raised an eyebrow, removed a gold ring with a bezel of lapis lazuli from his finger and held it up.

"Agreed," Pawero said quickly.

"The boy comes with me now, and you will go to the temple of Amun tomorrow morning and execute a bill of sale before witnesses."

Pawero was bowing over and over. "Yes, great one. Of course, of course. And what name shall I give for the buyer?"

"Meren."

The man stopped bowing and stared. Meren ignored him and continued. "Mark what I say, Pawero. From this day you have nothing to do with this boy. Do not come to my house seeking to trade on your shared blood. I have no wish to see you again." Without waiting for Pawero's reply, Meren motioned to Kysen.

"Come with me, child."

The boy followed him back across the square, but faltered as they were about to turn a corner. He stood watching his father, and Meren waited. Pawero's attention was fixed on the gold ring. He rubbed it, held it up so that it caught the sun's rays, brought it close to see the design on the bezel. Then, without a glance at his son, he hurried away. Kysen's eyes filled with tears, but he didn't cry. His gaze remained on the spot where his father disappeared, and he blinked rapidly. Meren reached out to put his hand on the boy's shoulder, but Kysen jumped, twisted around to face him, braced for a blow. Meren lowered his hand.

"I won't strike you."

Kysen merely looked at him.

"There will be time enough for you to learn the truth of my words."

When the boy remained in his defensive stance, Meren stepped back from him to show his benign intentions. After a while Kysen straightened. Meren began to walk again.

"Come, Kysen. The gods have put you in my way. You're my responsibility now, and my first duty is to see that you get a bath."

"Bath! Rather get a beating."

He could still hear that outraged response all these years later. Meren felt a spasm of pain as he studied Kysen's motionless body and recalled his childhood aversion to bathing. What a battle it had been to convince him that he wouldn't drown if a servant poured water over him in the shower stall.

"Meren, you're not listening."

He looked up to find Anath and Bener watching him. Kysen hadn't moved.

"Yes?"

"Bener asked what all the commotion was," Anath said.

"I arrested the pirate Othrys. He gave Kysen wine to drink just before he fell ill. If he doesn't wake soon, I will use more severe persuasion to make him tell me what was in the wine."

Anath rose and joined him at the foot of the bed. "Then you suspect him?"

"I must," Meren said. "He may have been lying from the first, but he did say something that made me think he might be innocent. He claimed he could have killed me when I sought refuge with him when I was suspected of trying to kill pharaoh."

"But he couldn't be sure you hadn't told your family where you were," Anath said. "If you had, and he killed you, he would have been suspected. Had I been faced with the situation, I would have waited to make certain your death couldn't be traced to me."

"And by the time he was certain, I'd already contacted my charioteers. I see what you mean."

Anath put her palm against his cheek. "You look terrible, my love."

Meren turned and kissed her palm, suddenly weary. He couldn't remember how long it had been since he slept.

"I can't rest."

"I know a sleeping potion that will help," Anath said. "I learned it from a Babylonian witch."

"A witch? That doesn't sound good. Besides, I must remain awake for Kysen."

"Nonsense," she said as she left the room. "Bener and I

will watch over him and wake you at the first sign of a change in his condition. I'll prepare the mixture at once."

Meren was too exhausted to argue. His thoughts were sluggish, his heart weary from the agony of the last few days. He sat beside Bener, and they studied Kysen's features together.

"Father, I have to talk to you."

Pressing his fingertips to his temples, Meren said, "I won't argue with you anymore."

"I don't want to argue, I just want to ask you about Anath."

"Not now," he said.

"No, not about you and Anath. About her wealth."

"What about it?"

"Didn't you say you went to her house? You saw it, and her possessions. She has as much furniture and more jewels than we do."

Meren touched Kysen's forehead. It felt cool. "Anath is the Eyes of Babylon. The position requires wealth and accrues wealth."

"Oh," Bener said with a frown. "It's just that you always say you're suspicious when those of moderate means become suddenly wealthy."

Meren transferred his gaze to his daughter, noted her calculating expression, and sighed. "You're doing it again, working out puzzles. Leave it be. You're to confine your thoughts to appropriate matters, and Anath's prosperity isn't your concern."

"But, Father, you always say—"

"No!"

Bener jumped and gave him a hurt look.

"Forgive me, child, but I have no patience left after your abduction . . . and this." He swept his arm toward Kysen.

"Speak to me about your concerns when Kysen . . . if he . . ."
He couldn't finish.

Anath appeared holding a glazed blue bottle and dragged
him from the room. Meren allowed her to lead him to his
bedchamber because he was too exhausted to argue. He lay
down, but refused to drink the concoction she poured into
a cup of wine.

"I don't want to be insensible while Kysen is ill."

"Very well." Anath set the cup on the floor and climbed
into the bed with him. She picked it up again. "A small sip
will help you sleep without making you groggy."

He took one sip to please her, then settled back in her
arms. He turned his face so that he could smell her perfumed body, but even that exotic scent failed to penetrate
the numbness that had settled over him. Anath watched him
for a while before summoning a servant, who appeared with
her lute. She moved to a cushion beside the bed and
strummed the strings of the instrument. It was an old one
she'd had for years, made of the shell of a large tortoise.

Meren lay with his eyes open, staring at the ceiling and
listening to her play. Slowly, against his will, his eyes closed.
He should be questioning Othrys, hunting down the missing Dilalu, anything to avoid having to think of losing Kysen
as he almost lost Bener. The last thing he remembered before he slept was Anath's voice murmuring, quiet as the
north breeze.

Chapter 17

Meren woke with a start. He sat up, searching frantically for anything familiar, and found only blackness. His hands groped, and he found the bed. Still blind, he stumbled, hitting a post, and lurched away from it. A wave of dizziness made him bend over and brace himself. Taking long breaths, he slowly unbent and took cautious steps with his arms flung out in front of him. At last his hands found wood, and he pushed open a door.

To his relief a charioteer stood outside. He squeezed his eyes shut and opened them. His blurry vision cleared, and he hurried to Kysen's room, his heart pounding. His son was still imprisoned in his frightening slumber. Bener sat on a stool and half lay on the bed beside her brother, asleep. Was it his imagination, or did Ky seem paler? He could hardly see the boy's chest move with his breathing. Growing cold with alarm, Meren dropped to his knees, took Kysen's cold hand in his, and prayed to Amun to save his son.

As he muttered the prayer, a shadow crossed the path of light cast by a lamp beside the bed, and an arm came down on his shoulder. Meren froze in shock, then recognized the heavy gold signet ring carved with cartouches enclosing two names.

"Majesty?" Meren whispered. He sank to the floor.

"Get up, Meren. I came as soon as my duties allowed." Tutankhamun lowered himself to one knee beside Meren, his young face full of concern. "How is he?"

Meren stood and looked down at Kysen. "He hasn't moved since I lay him there. The physician says he can do nothing."

The king searched his face, then nodded at Meren's sleeping daughter. "This is the work of the same one who abducted Lady Bener?"

"Aye, majesty."

"Meren, you look like you've been through battle and lost."

"Thy majesty has great perception, and since Kysen was looking for the merchant Dilalu, it could be that he is the evil one we seek. But I'm not sure, and I dare not send anyone to hunt him right now. I've already captured the pirate Othrys, whom I suspect, and I shouldn't have done it. If he's the murderer, Kysen may suffer for my recklessness." They both studied Kysen for a few moments.

"When I thought you'd tried to kill me I sent for Kysen," Tutankhamun said quietly. "I tried to make him betray you. A useless attempt, I admit. He told me I might as well kill him, because he wasn't going to help me. I remember thinking how much I admired him for refusing to abandon you. One with a lesser heart might have tried to save himself."

Meren almost smiled. "Bravery has always come easily to him, majesty. The first time I saw him I was surprised to find so great a heart lodged in the body of one born so low."

"The gods choose certain men and endow them with extraordinary gifts," Tutankhamun said. "Like those who rose from the common ranks to become great architects or physicians. He will make a fine staff of old age for you, an admirable successor."

"If he lives," Meren whispered.

Just then Anath and Nebamun came in with one of the king's physicians, and at their entrance Bener woke. Meren told his daughter to get some rest, and the physicians began to examine Kysen again.

Meren schooled himself to watch his son fail to react to the prodding and handling.

"Meren," the king said. "You're doing no good here, and we must talk. We'll go to your office. Come, Anath."

Once in the room, Tutankhamun began prowling around, picking up a scribe's palette and setting it down, toying with a wooden penholder in the form of a hollow tube. Meren stood steeped in anxiety beside the master's dais. Threatening Othrys had been a stupid thing to do. He was allowing his fear to govern him, and Kysen could well lose his life because of it. Anath tried to comfort him, but her touch only increased his agitation. Setting his jaw, he refrained from snapping at her and took her hand from his arm.

Tutankhamun paused near them and tossed the penholder onto a document case. As if from a distance Meren saw that his hands were shaking. He should have remembered that pharaoh was suffering too, and trying hard to conceal it.

"Yet another attack on you," the king said in a voice that shook. "We must find this criminal before he murders your whole family. My majesty cannot allow such insolence."

Meren shook his head wearily. "I can do nothing more until Kysen . . ."

He couldn't go on. He was afraid to voice his hope. It was too fragile to bear being put into words. Anath again touched his arm gently as she murmured words of comfort. This time he didn't move away.

"I took a chance in grabbing Othrys because I was desperate, and it gained me nothing."

"Had I been faced with such a threat," the king said, "I would have captured those most likely to be guilty as you did. Besides, I doubt Othrys is the culprit in this case. From what you say about him, he's too clever to do the poisoning himself. But I don't understand why the killer would poison Kysen at all."

"He sent a message saying this was punishment for failing to do as I was ordered," Meren said. "Kysen was in the Caverns looking for Dilalu."

"But why attack your children?" Tutankhamun said as he wandered over to a stack of notes. He picked them up and began going through them. "If he's so desperate to prevent you from finding out who he is, the most certain remedy would be your death."

"Ah, but majesty, what would happen if the criminal did kill Meren?" Anath asked.

Tutankhamun looked up from reading a papyrus and considered, his features becoming blank. "I would close the gates, shut down the docks, and rake this city from one end to the other for anyone suspicious. Then I'd hand anyone I caught to General Horemheb for questioning." He smiled. "The general's methods aren't as subtle as Meren's but they're effective. I wouldn't release the city from my grip until I was satisfied."

"Thus ruining many an illicit enterprise," Anath said. "This drinker of blood has a network of interests, many located here, if I'm correct. To avoid bringing down thy majesty's wrath, he must go carefully."

"I didn't do as he wished, however," Meren said.

"True," Anath replied. "But if you had, someone else would have been blamed for the death of Queen Nefertiti, pharaoh would have been satisfied, and the drinker of blood could operate safely."

The king leafed through another stack of papyri. "And all these threats began the moment you returned from Horizon of the Aten."

"And the moment Kysen and Bener began their investigations of Prince Usermontu and Lord Pendua, majesty," Meren said. "I long to drag each suspect into a cell and beat them until I get a confession, but I dare not for fear there's some antidote Kysen needs that the criminal is withholding."

"Yes," the king said. He looked down at the records he was holding. "So instead you've been wading through old documents." He sighed and read the top sheet of papyrus. "By the mercy of Amun, look at these. It all seems so long ago, a lifetime. This is from year fifteen of my brother's reign, a record of cattle from the temple of Ra given to Usermontu for his loyal service. I was almost five." His eyes held a distant memory. "I haven't seen old Usermontu in years. The last time was just before the queen died, I think. Yes, I remember she gave him an audience, and berated him as if he were a disobedient monkey for falsifying some kind of record."

Meren drew closer. "Thy majesty never told me."

"I had forgotten until I saw this." The king pointed to the document he held. "I didn't understand the details, but I remember the violence of their quarrel. I had never heard a servant raise his voice to a member of the royal family before, and Usermontu was so furious he was spewing his words along with quite a bit of spittle."

"What did her majesty do?"

"I don't know," Tutankhamun said, his gaze growing clouded as he tried to recall. "I'm not sure, but—yes, I think she became ill before she did anything to him." Tutankhamun's head drooped, and he allowed the document to fall to the floor. "Then she died, and I was alone."

"Usermontu," Meren said. "I never did like him."

Anath said, "You're not alone."

"You think he could have killed the queen to prevent her from exposing him?" Tutankhamun asked.

"It's possible, majesty," Anath replied. "He seems to have been the most corrupt of her servants."

Meren tried to evaluate what the king had told him, but his heart was back in the sickroom with Kysen. Nothing mattered, not even Nefertiti's death, as long as his son was in danger. The reason and clarity that usually governed his thoughts seemed to have vanished. In its place terror ruled, and now that old burning feeling in his chest had returned, the feeling he got when he'd missed something important. He nearly swore aloud as the agitation over this failure combined with the fear to make his state almost unbearable. He roused from this state of dazed misery when the king spoke to him.

"I must go," the boy said. "You're distracted and miserable, and nothing I can say will help."

"Majesty, thy presence has been a great comfort."

"I think not." Tutankhamun drew near and searched Meren's face. "Is this the torment a parent endures when his child suffers?"

"Yes, Golden One. There is no worse pain."

"Ankhesenamun is with child."

Anath smoothly stepped into the small silence. "We rejoice with thy majesty."

"Indeed," Meren said. "Amun be praised."

Tutankhamun nodded gravely. "I will intercede with the god, my father, on Kysen's behalf."

At that moment Bener rushed in, barely able to contain herself long enough to kneel when she saw the king.

"He's awake!"

Everyone rushed to Kysen's room, including the king. Meren hurtled to the bed, and dropped to his knees.

"Ky?"

Kysen opened his eyes briefly, then closed them. "I feel so odd."

He opened his eyes again and tried to get up. Meren grabbed his shoulders and pushed him down again.

"Nebamun says you mustn't get up yet."

"What happened?"

"Someone poisoned you."

"Marduk! *Ow*, my head."

Nebamun appeared with a cup of water. Meren held it while Kysen drank. After a few sips he sighed and lay back.

"There's something I must tell . . ." Kysen's eyes closed, and his voice faded.

Meren shook his son. "Kysen!"

"Fear not, lord," Nebamun said as he steadied his patient against Meren's frantic shaking. "This is a natural sleep, not one induced by poison."

With relief Meren released Kysen, rose and turned to find that the king had slipped away.

"His majesty felt you needed rest now that Kysen is out of danger," Anath said.

Meren walked to the end of the bed and stood gazing on his son. He didn't know how long he spent measuring the depth of Kysen's breathing, his coloring, his posture. Eventually he was able to believe the physician's happy pronouncement. Anath waited patiently beside him, and at last he smiled at her. With Kysen out of danger it was as if his heart had been suddenly freed. His thoughts became clearer, and at the same time that grating sensation of having forgotten something rose to prominence.

"I wish pharaoh hadn't left," Meren said to Anath. "Something he said bothered me."

"About Usermontu?"

"I'm not sure," Meren said. He gazed at Kysen for a few moments, then realized he wasn't doing any good here. "Come," he said to Anath. With a last glance at Kysen, they left the bedchamber.

"What did pharaoh say that disturbed you?" Anath asked as they walked.

"I wish I knew. For weeks now I've felt I've missed something important. If I could only remember what it is, I might have the key to this whole mystery."

"You're tired," Anath said as they walked into the reception hall. "Why not go to bed and think about it tomorrow when you're refreshed?"

"No," Meren said. He walked around the dais, his head bent, his thoughts released from their prison of fear. "No, I can almost see it. It will come to me, but not if I sleep."

Anath folded her arms and watched him. "If you must push yourself to exhaustion, at least get some air. You've been cooped up in the house too long. No wonder your thoughts hide from you. Your heart is choking on stale humors."

Rolling his shoulders to ease the ache in them, Meren sighed. "You're right. Sitting around will do no good. We'll take my chariot."

"Good, then you can drive me to my house. I promised Bener some resins she wants to use for a healing incense for Kysen."

It didn't take long before they were driving out of the gates of Golden House. The chariot clattered over ruts in the street, and Wind Chaser and Star Chaser snorted and tossed their heads in the chill air of early morning. Meren welcomed the drive. Guiding the chariot, allowing his hands to feel the mood of the horses through the reins, these familiar activities allowed his heart the freedom to open to any drift of memory, any small eddy of thought that might spark the key recollection. Unfortunately the trip wasn't long enough, and he was still preoccupied as they walked into the house.

Anath vanished in the direction of the kitchen, and Meren wandered through the house. He stepped around a couch made of ebony and decorated with bands of gold and passed several chairs of the finest cedar. Brilliantly colored hangings covered the walls, and in a side room he glimpsed serving vessels of silver. He wandered onto a loggia that afforded a view of a reflection pool the size of a small lake.

If he couldn't resolve this matter of the queen's killer soon, he might have to resort to the king's methods and seal the city, apprehend all the suspected ones, and interrogate them until one of them broke. He desperately wished to avoid such a course, for the search would take days, during which his family would be at risk no matter how he protected them. Allowing his thoughts to roam freely was the best way to encourage the spark of recollection.

Something in that conversation with the king and Anath had provoked that burning feeling in his chest, that feeling of having almost glimpsed the solution. Not the part about Usermontu. Something else. There had been a discussion of the reasoning behind Bener's abduction and Kysen's poisoning. Meren leaned against a column and lifted his face to the north breeze as his thoughts drifted.

The king's praise of Kysen had been small comfort while his son had been in danger, but now he could enjoy the fact that pharaoh had a good opinion of him. Tutankhamun admired strength, to a certain degree. He didn't admire strength that pitted itself against him, and he was highly suspicious. That was why he remarked upon the fact that Meren's troubles began the moment he returned from Horizon of the Aten. But Meren had learned over the years that just because two things happened around the same time didn't always mean they were related.

It was unfortunate that Tutankhamun had been so young when the queen died, for his clever heart would have been of great help. He might have understood more about the quarrel between the queen and Usermontu. But the king had been a child. What had he said? He'd been five in the fifteenth year of Akhenaten. Pharaoh had been reading through those records—the old tallies of foreign tribute, the orders for rations for slaves belonging to the Aten temple, that transfer of deed for the land old Thanuro never lived to enjoy.

His thoughts slowed, and Meren pushed himself away from the column, his gaze fixed on a stand of reeds in the lake. Like a leopard crouched in tall grass he waited while a piece of information from one place, and a fact from another drifted together with inconsequential remarks from yet another source. Not daring to move, hardly breathing, he held still while his view of certain events shifted with the suddenness of a whip stroke.

At last, his heart racing, he whispered, "Damnation."

"There you are." Anath walked onto the loggia holding a small cloth bundle. "I found the resin."

"*Damnation, Anath.*" Meren was still staring at the reeds.

"What is it?" she asked, staring at the lake. "I don't see anything."

He looked at her then, and she went still.

"What?" she said with a sharpness that woke him from his stunned trance.

"By the gods!" He slapped the column. "It was there all along, and I didn't see it."

"Meren, you're not making sense."

"The transfer of the deed to Thanuro's land. The gift from pharaoh." He grabbed Anath. "The transfer was recorded in year sixteen of Akhenaten's reign."

"Yes, I know."

"Anath, Thanuro died in year fifteen."

There was a small pause. Then Anath said lightly, "No, I don't think so."

"I'm certain of it. I've been over those cursed documents too many times. Even the script is engraved in my memory. The deed was finalized a year after the priest was supposed to have died. Which means either someone took the land pretending to be him, or he never died at all."

"It's merely a confusion," Anath said. "There are thousands of such transfers every year, and some of them are bound to be wrong."

"Ordinarily I'd agree," Meren said. "But not this time, because two things happened the year before that transfer. Thanuro died. And Zulaya appeared in Egypt."

"So did many people."

"You still don't understand. Remember what Yamen told me about his murderer when he was dying? He said, 'He'll sacrifice you as he does all who know him.'" Meren clapped his hands in excitement. "And then he said something that has always bothered me. He said, 'He is in my heart. There is no other who knows him.' That phrase always seemed familiar, but I didn't place it until just now. Then I remembered that not long ago the king was reading Akhenaten's hymn to the Aten."

Anath's brow wrinkled and she shook her head.

"Don't you see? Those are Akhenaten's words, written about his relationship to the Aten. Yamen was telling me that the guilty one made sacrifices and recited Aten hymns. He was a priest. Thanuro." Meren prowled the loggia as he thought, murmuring to himself. "And Thanuro is Zulaya."

He stopped, staring out into the painful brightness of the garden. Suddenly years dropped away, and he was back at Horizon of the Aten, and memories, obscured by pain and deliberate forgetting, cleared to the definition of a newly painted fresco. He was walking through the royal courts, the temple gateways, the queen's palace, glancing at a priest, then moving on, concerned with his own survival, giving the man little thought. This man whom the queen distrusted, this priest, like all others, shaved his head, his eyebrows, his face. He wore the garb of a priest, and affected the stately demeanor of one who dealt with a god.

Meren heard Anath speaking to him, but he held up a hand for silence. He'd only seen Zulaya once, briefly, and then it had been in a dark, crowded tavern. Could it be? Meren tried to fit the image of the priest with that of the merchant. Zulaya was older than the man Meren remembered. He no longer shaved his head, eyebrows, and face. He wore the raiment of a foreigner, even the hairstyle of an Asiatic. The difference was just drastic enough to conceal an identity no longer of any use. Meren felt Anath's hand on his arm and dragged his attention back to her.

"You're certain Zulaya is the priest Thanuro?" Anath's confused smile faded. She held Meren's gaze for a long time. "Yes, I can see that you are."

"Of course I'm certain. Don't you see it too?"

Anath dropped the resin bundle and shook her head. "Oh, my dear love. I'm so sorry."

"It's not your fault. None of us noticed the discrepancy in the dates."

She walked toward the doorway that led to the reception hall, turned, and looked at him sorrowfully. "No, Meren. I'm sorry you noticed it at all. Father?"

A tall shadow appeared in the doorway, cast by a figure approaching from the lamplit hall. Meren took a step back as Zulaya neared, followed by half a dozen armed men. Zulaya was holding Khufu, stroking his patched fur as he regarded Meren. Looking from Anath to Zulaya, Meren's eyes widened. Pain followed his confusion, then he smothered his emotions. In the space between one heartbeat and another Meren went from elation to misery and fury, and on to battle readiness.

Zulaya inclined his head. "I trust your son has recovered by now, Lord Meren."

Meren transferred his gaze to Anath, his heart pounding as he stalled for time. "Your father is dead."

"My mother told me who my real father was when I was six," Anath said. "Did you really think a man as aged as Nebwawi could sire a child? He was an arrogant fool to believe it, but then, he never bothered to wonder about anything having to do with my mother or me."

"None of this is relevant to our problem of the moment," Zulaya said.

Meren eyed the men who had moved around him to form a half circle. "Now I understand your habit of elusiveness while you're in Egypt, Zulaya, although I don't think anyone would recognize you in your present guise. You're the Aten priest, Thanuro."

"That's not important."

"True, Zulaya. What's important is that you bribed the steward Wah to poison the great royal wife Nefertiti, and for that you will die."

Zulaya stroked Khufu and said, "My dear Lord Meren, you're in no position to speak of who is going to die."

Chapter 18

Bener carried a bowl of soup and a wooden spoon into the house from the kitchens, her spirits light with relief at her brother's awakening. Kysen's illness had frightened her as much as being abducted. She paused to blow on the soup, for it was too hot to be consumed. Chunks of heron meat floated in the broth along with cabbage and beans. Kysen liked heron, and she'd ordered the soup prepared hoping to tempt him. He'd rested after Father left with Anath, but he was awake now.

She paused in her cooling efforts to look over her shoulder. A charioteer lurked at a distance, her ever-present companion when she wasn't with Anath. Who was it? Bener scowled as she recognized Lord Irzanen. That arrogant son of a sow had ruined her plans to charm incriminating admissions out of Lord Usermontu's son. It was beyond her understanding why he thought he had a right to interfere. Besides, if she hadn't been forced to take him to task for his rudeness, she wouldn't have been captured by that enormous dark creature with the knife.

No, don't dwell upon it. Her sleep was invaded by demons, her dreams bizarre versions of the endless hours spent in that tiny, airless room. Bener swallowed hard to rid herself of tears that would betray weakness. She'd never contemplated dying, never really known what it was to fear for her life until she was abducted. Now she understood why Father was always so concerned for her welfare. But the trouble hadn't been her fault. Father's enemy was far more clever and powerful than any he'd ever fought. That was the crux of the matter.

It wasn't fair. In spite of the ordeal, Bener knew she could be of help if everyone would stop treating her as if she was lackwitted. All her efforts to help Father had come to ruin because of the abduction. No one would remember her clever heart now that she'd nearly gotten killed, and Father was too frightened of losing her to admit she had been making progress. If she'd continued with her investigations, she would have discovered the most secret of secrets Pendua and Usermontu possessed.

Now she wouldn't be allowed even to read royal dispatches, much less do anything adventurous. Bener scowled at Irzanen, who reddened and looked away. Turning her back on the young man, she blew on the soup again and proceeded through the reception hall. As she passed the master's dais she saw a small wicker box. Setting the soup down she picked it up and opened it to reveal the piece of bone Father had found at the well where poor old Satet had drowned. Bener sighed, thinking of the lively old woman whose goose still terrorized the kitchen yard. Neither Kysen, nor Bener or Meren, were willing to believe Satet simply fell into the well, but so far no witness to the contrary had been located.

Bener closed the box lid, slipped the container under her arm, and took the soup to Kysen's room. Her brother was sitting in bed with his back propped against the headboard of polished cedar inlaid with ivory. Bener handed the soup to Kysen. When he'd finished half of it, she produced the wicker box and lifted the lid.

"I found this in the hall."

Kysen glanced at the fragment. "Father told you not to interfere."

"I'm not interfering. I want to know where to put it."

"Give it to me."

Bener put the box on top of a chest. "You don't need it. Nebamun said you wouldn't be able to remain awake for long, and I can see you're already tired from holding the soup bowl."

"I may look tired, but I can't sleep," Kysen said. "I'm weary of sleeping. I've done too much of it."

Bener regarded him for a moment. His face had lost most of its color, and his eyes seemed twice as large as they'd been before his illness, probably because of the hollows under them and in his cheeks.

"I'll play for you," she said. Then she smiled. "You always told me my music put you to sleep."

Kysen looked embarrassed. "Sorry."

"I think I saw Anath's lute outside Father's rooms."

Bener hurried down the corridor that led to the master's suite, retrieved the instrument, and returned to find Kysen had lain down again. She sat on a cushion beside him and strummed the lute. Sooner or later she was going to persuade Father to speak of his relationship with Anath. She liked the Eyes of Babylon, who had the kind of adventures for which Bener longed. But Anath had changed since her last stay at home. She seemed more deliberately charming and far more biddable than Bener remembered.

To put Kysen at ease Bener played an old tune said to

have been composed in the time of the pyramid builders, a slow, soft melody. Then she played one her sister Isis had composed. As she finished she shifted the lute to a more comfortable position, and something caught on her gown. The body of the instrument had been constructed from a large tortoise shell, and when she reversed the instrument she found a jagged hole in it.

"Son of a she-goat!"

Kysen jerked and opened his eyes. "Huh?"

"Look at this."

She thrust the lute at him and jumped to her feet. Snatching the wicker box, she grabbed the piece of bone, took it to Kysen, and fitted it into the hole in the tortoise shell.

"It's tortoise shell," she said.

They looked at each other.

"Anath," Bener whispered. "Remember the night Satet was killed? I'd commissioned those musicians to play for Father again to help him relax and rest."

"You think she concealed herself among them?"

"But why would she kill the old woman?" Bener dropped the tortoise shell fragment and looked at Kysen. "Oh, no."

Kysen pounded the bed. "Where is she?"

"Father took her home to fetch something."

They exchanged horrified glances. Kysen shoved the lute away and struggled to get out of bed. Bener grabbed his shoulder.

"No, you're too weak."

"I have to——"

Bener gave him a hard shove. "I'll do it." She ran to the door and spotted Irzanen, who came alert at her sudden appearance.

"What's wrong, lady?"

"Find Abu and Reia. Summon every man."

"But—"

Bener wasn't Lord Meren's daughter for nothing. She pulled herself up and lowered her voice an octave.

"Summon the charioteers at once, or by all the gods I'll see you condemned to the farthest desert mine in the empire!"

Irzanen vanished, and Bener returned to Kysen. Her brother was trying to get out of bed. Cursing under her breath, Bener helped him stand, and they began to walk to the hall.

"He hasn't been gone long," she said as they walked.

"We must go carefully," Kysen said. "Father is safe as long as she doesn't know we've discovered her crime. Gods, Bener, what evil do we confront that perverts even the Eyes of Babylon?"

"She's in the pay of the murderer, and she's been spying on us all along. Think about it. No wonder Father came upon her that morning. She'd been here all along to kill Satet."

"I'll go to her house," Kysen said as they entered the hall. "You stay here in case we miss them and they come back. I'll leave Irzanen and Reia with you."

Bener opened her mouth, but shut it again when she read the expression on Kysen's face. It wasn't long before she was standing at the front door watching chariot after chariot clatter along the avenue and through the gates. She waved dust out of her face. Biting her lip, she sat down on the top step and fixed her gaze on the street beyond the open gate, and waited.

Meren said nothing as Zulaya stared into his eyes with a hungry excitement that was as disturbing as the peril to which his folly had led him. He had always liked Anath, and her years of expertise and proven service had made him trust her from the first. Lulled by friendship and trust, his habitual wariness had failed to warn him against her, and he'd succumbed to a seduction so obvious he blushed to remember it.

Despite his experience, he, who had scoffed at men whose passions made them foolish, had been blinded by a woman's charm and daring. Yet he should have recognized the hints—how she'd inserted herself into his investigation, how she'd tried to delay his questioning of Sebek. At Horizon of the Aten she had directed him to a place she probably knew would contain no evidence that could harm her father. At every turn she'd encouraged him to suspect anyone but Zulaya. She had been against questioning the merchant, and she'd urged him to submit to the abductor's demands once Bener had been taken.

"I think our discussion should be held inside," Zulaya said. He set Khufu down and went into the hall.

Meren followed him, but not before one of the guards relieved him of his dagger. Anath walked past him without a glance to confront her father.

"This is madness. You should have let me kill him long ago, when it became clear he wasn't going to be manageable."

Zulaya sat on the master's dais, picked up grapes from a side table and popped one in his mouth. "You were always so impatient, little jewel. I haven't spoken with him, and already you foretell disappointment. I admit I wasn't planning to meet our guest until we poisoned his son for the second time, but we must all put up with little disruptions and inconveniences."

Meren almost shivered as the complexity and ruthlessness of Zulaya's intentions became clear. Struggling to hide how shocked and off balance he was, he tried to keep his features arranged in a facade of mild surprise. He could see little resemblance between Anath and Zulaya. Only a slight hint in the way their eyes tilted at the outside corners. No, their resemblance lay not so much in features as in their easy manner, an air of self-reliance, and a daring that was coldly calculating and never escalated into recklessness.

To give himself time to think, Meren walked up to the foot of the dais stairs and asked, "The queen found out you were keeping the spoils of the temples you looted for the Aten, didn't she? That's why you had to risk murdering the great royal wife. But you had to trust old Wah, the steward, to help you, and he was weak. Was that why you decided to vanish? Why didn't you simply kill him?"

"I should have," Zulaya said as he pulled another grape from its stalk, "but he was such a little squirrel of a man. He lived in terror of me, so much so that he caused me little concern." He leaned back in his chair and contemplated the ceiling. "After the queen was dead it would have been foolish to kill him and arouse suspicion. And later I had"— Zulaya's expression darkened—"I had other concerns that forced me to leave Horizon of the Aten. And certainly Wah had no wish to reveal his guilt and thus mine. But how was I to know he'd eventually grow confident enough to seek advancement at court again and turn to your sister to do it? I should have remembered how much he craved the glory of royal favor and patronage."

"You haven't answered my first question. Were you taking the temple riches for yourself?"

Zulaya grinned at Anath. "Ah, you see, my little jewel, what comes of being forced to keep company with men like Ay, Maya, and Horemheb? Men of stunted vision and pruned imagination. Even Meren's clever heart has suffered from the contamination."

"Get on with it, Father. He'll be missed soon."

"You still haven't answered my question," Meren said.

"I will tell you something far more important, my dear Lord Meren, something you may understand, for we're alike, you and I. The world is filled with seekers of wealth, people who will do things that would make an ordinary man vomit, in order to obtain what you and I have. And most of them are like your friends and the other kicking, biting, and scratching place-seekers at court. Once they climb high enough to obtain riches, they stagnate in their own mediocrity. They never understand that the ultimate gratification comes from power. Do you not feel it every time you force someone to do your bidding against his will? There is such pleasure in being able to twist a heart, to distort it until a man or woman becomes something else entirely."

Meren had to look at Anath. "Is that what he did to you?"

"No!" Anath pressed her lips together and turned her head.

Zulaya patted her arm. "Of course not. I always told my little jewel the truth. Of what use would it be to lie to my blood?" His expression softened. "Remember the old saying that when one is in a strange house, beware of approaching the women? I never agreed with it, and one day I met Anath's mother. She was the only woman I ever loved, and she belonged to an old man." Zulaya appeared lost in sad memories, but the darkness in his eyes vanished as he gazed at Anath. "My little jewel is my successor, my beloved child. She must know everything."

"Why else do you think I would seek to become one of the Eyes and Ears of Pharaoh?" Anath hissed. She walked down the steps until she stood on the last one, her eyes level with Meren's. "Do you think I wanted to go to Babylon, to live away from the Two Lands? You may enjoy listening to the lies and bickering of foreigners, but I do not. I had to escape Nebwawi, and Father thought it was a way to advance our interests. So I became the Eyes of Babylon."

"To be close to your dear father."

"And to learn the ways of power," Zulaya said. "Don't be hurt, Meren. Anath is fond of you. She told me so."

He had no wish to expose himself further to Zulaya or his bitch of a daughter. "Yet again you fail to tell me why you killed the queen."

"You have the answer if you think carefully, but we have more pressing business to discuss. I trust your son is better now."

Meren could feel the burn of desire, the desire to strangle Zulaya until his eyes bled. "You know he is."

"Good," Zulaya said cheerfully. "Then you will wish to keep him that way."

"If you're threatening him in order to make me do what you want, come out with it!" Meren could have bitten his tongue. He'd revealed his frustration and alarm, exposing his weakness to this viper. Zulaya was smiling at him like a concubine with a newborn son.

"How indelicate of you, my dear Lord Meren. The strain of your recent troubles is beginning to show. Would you like some wine? Perhaps a cup will calm you."

"Cease this wordplay," Meren said. "What do you want?"

Zulaya set his grapes down, leaned toward Meren, and seemed to drink in the vision of his enemy standing beneath him. "Can't you guess? I want you, Meren. I want to hold you in my hand, to govern your conduct, to determine your plans, and most of all I want to control the man who

calls himself Friend of the King. I propose an alliance between us. A fair trade for the lives of your children, I think."

"I do your bidding or you kill my family," Meren said
with a sneer.

Zulaya waved a hand. "I wouldn't have phrased it so tact-
lessly, but you're right. Think carefully on the advantages of
such an alliance. I can deliver many enemies into your hands."

"What you describe isn't an alliance, it's slavery."

"If you choose to view it that way. You could think of
it as an alliance between yourself and a man of greater
power."

"I'm not in the habit of deceiving myself, Zulaya."

Anath threw up her hands. "This is absurd, Father. He'll
agree with whatever you propose, and the moment he's free
he'll attack."

"My little jewel, you're absolutely right, and that's what
I'd expect him to do."

"But you've devised a remedy," Meren said.

Inclining his head, Zulaya chuckled. "You're beginning to
understand me at last, my dear Lord Meren. Yes, I have a
remedy. Several. Let me see. Ah, I remember now. Did you
know that your brother, whom I believe you call Ra, has
been falsifying the estimates of crop yields on his lands for
over ten years? Did you know that your sister Idut's son has
fathered a child by the daughter of Prince Setau? The girl
is only twelve, I'm afraid, and her father had planned to
marry her to Maya's oldest son next year. Then there's the
matter of your cousin Ebana, whom you love as a brother.
I fear he has done things in the past that would cause pharaoh
to have him flayed alive.

"There was something else." Zulaya picked up some grapes
and studied them as if finding the juiciest was more important than talking to Meren. "Oh, yes, now I remember."

He picked out a grape and chewed it thoughtfully. "If any-thing happens to me, I've made rather complicated arrange-ments so that your son and all three of your daughters will die. Slowly, and in agony."

Meren simply looked at Zulaya without responding.

As the silence lengthened, Anath began to twist one of the electrum rings she wore. "I was against this from the beginning, and now you see why. He's not broken or afraid. He'll agree to anything, then go to pharaoh and betray us, just as he did when you abducted Bener."

"And I repeat, my jewel, that it doesn't matter what he did before. The abduction and the poisoning were merely exhibitions, a way to make Meren realize how defenseless he is. Henceforth he'll conduct himself with honor toward us, because he knows of a certainty what will happen should he do otherwise." Zulaya cocked his head to the side and gave Meren a gentle smile. "You do believe me about what will happen to your children, don't you, my lord?"

Meren closed his eyes and nodded. He had never been faced with so brilliant a heart combined with such ruthless evil. His every move had been foreseen and checked, his es-cape routes blocked. For months now he'd been struggling as if he were a beetle drowning in honey, never quite grasp-ing the nature of his enemy until it was too late. And now he'd managed to endanger his children. Suddenly Meren felt a devastating terror combined with an equally overwhelm-ing weariness of spirit. He opened his eyes and said, "Yes, I believe you."

"Good," Zulaya said. He rose and came down the steps to Meren. "Then I need not provide further proof of my power to destroy them."

"No."

Without warning Meren had a vision of Kysen, Bener,

Tefnut, and Isis, lying on embalmer's tables, their naked bodies desiccated, stitched together, awaiting the mummy bandages. He heard Zulaya's voice, felt someone take his arm.

"Easy, Meren," his captor said as he took Meren's arm. "You've taxed yourself too much lately, and after all, you must admit you were never up to a fight with me, and defeat has brought you low."

Wishing he could stab the man with his own dagger, Meren barely restrained himself as Zulaya led him to a couch and made him sit. The vision was gone, but its effect remained, and Meren cursed his momentary weakness.

"Fear not," Zulaya said as he poured a cup of water and handed it to Meren. "You don't have to manage everything alone. I had my men follow Kysen earlier, and they should have abducted him at the Divine Lotus, but Dilalu turned coward at having to face your men and bungled the whole thing. Fortunately I took advantage of the situation and provided a hiding place to him where he could be safe from you and the others he thinks are after him."

"No doubt you helped him along in this belief that someone is trying to kill him."

"Of course. And now I've arranged for certain incriminating documents to be found in the house as well. You, my friend, will raid Dilalu's hiding place. He will be killed in the fight, and you'll recover the proof that the old ruffian was behind the death of the great royal wife."

"I'm not going to murder him," Meren snapped. His best hope was to pretend weakness and submission until he saw a clear path by which to escape Zulaya's clutches.

"Oh, you needn't do it yourself," Zulaya said. "Later we'll discuss a few changes in the way you conduct the affairs of the Eyes and Ears of Pharaoh."

"What changes?"

"Nothing drastic. Mere changes in staff. A few of your charioteers need replacing, especially Abu and the one called Reia. I have excellent men in mind to replace them. But we'll speak of this later. The most important change is that you're going to marry my little jewel."

"No!" Meren shouted.

Anath echoed him. "Father, no!"

Zulaya waved his hands. "Now, don't argue, either of you. I've made the decision, and there's no use objecting." He gave them a beneficent smile. "I know there's an attraction between you."

"Not anymore," Meren said. "And I'm not accustomed to having anyone dictate to me on so personal a matter."

Zulaya drew near, his gaze hardening. "You'll have to learn, unless you prefer risking the life of that beautiful daughter of yours who's visiting her elder sister at the moment. What is she called? Ah, yes. Isis."

Meren gripped the edge of the couch and willed himself to appear defeated. He lowered his head. "Very well."

"It doesn't matter if he agrees because I don't."

"You'll see reason," Zulaya said. "But there are more pressing tasks to perform at the moment." He grabbed Meren's arm, pulled him to his feet, and shoved him. "Come, my dear Lord Meren. It's time to hunt down and destroy the murderer of Queen Nefertiti."

Chapter 19

Meren stepped outside with Zulaya and Anath right behind him. Only two chariots stood in the forecourt, bathed in the clean sunlight of early morning. Meren was glad to see Wind Chaser and Star Chaser still waiting for him, but he hid his surprise when Zulaya dismissed the guards that had insured his cooperation. Meren had been struck by how certain Zulaya was of his power, indeed had deliberately fostered it by his passive reaction. Still, there was a guard, a man who appeared around the corner of the house and saluted Zulaya. As he neared, Meren began to understand why Zulaya felt his presence sufficient.

This was a young man of unusual and pleasing appearance. Taller than any but a Nubian, strong, agile with the coordination that comes from a life spent in warfare. He had auburn-tinted dark hair that grew long, almost to his shoulders, and brown eyes that glittered in the sunlight. The closer he came the more certain Meren was that this was no ordinary hired ruffian; he'd seen that flat, reptilian blankness of expression a few times in his life. The eyes looked as if some artisan had placed false glass ones in a living man's head. The muscles of the cheeks and mouth seemed rigid, like stretched leather. When the young man turned his gaze on Meren their eyes met, and Meren felt that instantaneous evaluation. It consisted of two categories—those who were prey, and those who were not. The glass eyes moved on, leaving Meren with the certainty that he was one of the prey.

This, then, was the reason for Zulaya's confidence. Meren was sure of it. Just as he was certain that the young man with the glass eyes and frozen expression of a cobra was a trained assassin.

Zulaya stepped into his chariot and said, "Nebra, you're here at last. We can proceed."

Nebra gave his master a chilly smile, drew a knife and touched Meren's side with its tip. "Take the reins, my lord."

Meren got into the vehicle and picked up the reins as Anath joined her father. He glimpsed a flash of mottled gray and black, and Khufu leaped aboard with his mistress. Nebra stood beside Meren with one arm gripping the chariot rail nearest his captive. He'd draped the knife hand with a cloak he'd placed over his arm, but kept the point touching Meren's side.

He was ordered to drive at a modest pace, with Nebra directing his course and Zulaya and Anath following. Meren searched his surroundings as he drove, for it was clear they would meet more guards before attacking Dilalu. If he was going to escape before Zulaya forced him to participate in a murder, it would have to be soon. They skirted the edge of the Caverns, walking the horses through streets filled with pedestrians—women on their way to the river with baskets of laundry, farmers riding donkeys laden with produce, herdsmen whose sheep and pigs scuttled through the streets on the way to butchers.

Meren didn't see any opportunity to escape until they were far enough away from Anath's house to prevent Zulaya from calling for help. Soon the streets they took were too narrow to afford room to maneuver. Meren grew more anxious the longer they drove. Dilalu's hiding place had to be close, and he must take a chance quickly.

At last the crooked lane on which they traveled opened into a busy market in space surrounded by workshops and storehouses. Stalls topped with palm branches cluttered every surface, and there wasn't much room for the chariots. Nebra drew nearer and pressed the knifepoint into Meren's flesh when a flower seller thrust a garland at him. Meren shook his head and guided the chariot away from her. Behind them Zulaya snarled at the woman as she tried the same trick with him. When Nebra ordered him to go around an old man selling sandals from a basket, Meren turned Wind and Star to the left, but gave the reins a tiny flick. The horses danced sideways, causing the chariot to wrench, but Nebra kept his footing.

Meren cursed his ill luck as he maneuvered through the stalls and pedestrians. Their route was so circuitous that they doubled back and ended up at right angles to Zulaya and Anath. The old sandal vendor had blocked the chariot and was hawking his wares, oblivious to Zulaya's threats. Finally Zulaya gave the reins to Anath, and got out of the vehicle to rid himself of the old man.

Meren scoured the market for a way to distract Nebra. He was contemplating startling the green monkey sitting on the roof of a cloth stall when he glimpsed Khufu out of the corner of his eye. The scarred feline was sitting beside Zulaya's chariot and wore an air of frenzied anticipation

Meren knew well. He braced himself as Zulaya walked back
to the vehicle. Khufu's paw shot out. There was a hiss, and
dirty claws sank into Zulaya's foot. Zulaya cried out, and
for a mere instant Nebra's predatory attention faltered.

At the same time Meren's elbow jabbed into his gut. He
wrenched around, gripped Nebra's wrist, and twisted it as
his captor thrust with the knife. Meren bashed Nebra's hand
against the side of the chariot. The cloak over the assassin's
arm fell, but the blow failed to jar the weapon loose. He
kneed Meren in the stomach and lashed out with his foot.
Meren took the blows and nearly lost his grip on the knife
hand. Gasping for breath, he felt Nebra heave, and he was
thrown off balance. He heard Zulaya's voice, and knew he
had no time left. Releasing Nebra suddenly, he braced with
both arms and rammed the young man with both feet. As
he did so vendors and customers alike ran from the com-
batants, stumbling and screaming. The green monkey
screeched, jumped onto the chariot where Anath was trying
to control the startled horses, and slapped at Khufu with
its tiny hands.

Nebra hurtled backward from the chariot and hit Zulaya
as he ran toward the fighters. The knife flew from the assassin's hand at the impact and landed under the chariot.
Before either man could recover, Meren jumped down and
fished under the vehicle for the knife. With an economy of
movement Nebra rolled off Zulaya and to his feet and drew
a dagger, all in one motion. Nebra took but a heartbeat to
draw back his arm, wearing an expression of casual mastery.
All this he did in the time it took Meren to find the knife
and Zulaya to get to his feet.

Meren saw Nebra's movements as a blur. He was holding the assassin's knife by the handle. Without thinking, in
that state of supreme alertness that battle induced, he drew

the knife back so that his forearm blocked his lower face and threw it with a slashing, diagonal movement. The blade impaled Nebra through the eye, and his hands came up to grip it before he tottered and fell. As he did, Zulaya leaped over his body and planted himself in front of Meren, knife in hand. He shook his head.

"I have been foolish, it seems."

"Yes," Anath said.

Meren looked over his shoulder to find her behind him, also armed with a blade. His gaze darted from one to the other as they drew their knives back, preparing for the kill. All at once there was a high-pitched squeal, a growling hiss, and the green monkey scampered across the empty space created by their fight with Khufu in pursuit. The creature glanced over its shoulder, saw Khufu gaining, and scrambled up Zulaya's leg to perch on his shoulders.

Anath threw her knife as Khufu clawed his way up after the monkey. Meren dodged it, and the blade impaled Zulaya in the chest as he stood struggling with the cat and the monkey. Frightened by the blow, the animals sprang off Zulaya. Anath cried out and rushed to her father with Meren close behind. He grabbed her, but she twisted out of his grip and threw herself down beside the wounded man. Sobbing uncontrollably, Anath tried to staunch the blood that flowed from the wound around the knife.

Meren knelt on the other side of Zulaya, shoved Anath, and gripped the man's face. "You're dying. Tell me what you planned for my family, Zulaya. Don't go to the underworld with more evil to weight down your ka."

Zulaya gasped, panting, and his lips twisted into a grimace.

Meren gripped him hard. "Zulaya, tell me!"

Around them the sound of panic lessened when foot soldiers entered the market from several directions. Trumpets blared, but Meren paid no attention.

Anath thrust Meren aside and gathered Zulaya in her arms.

"Father, Father, I didn't mean to—" she choked and sobbed again.

Zulaya's color was fading rapidly, and his voice was weak. "No, my little jewel, of course you did not. No matter, no matter."

"Do something!" Anath screamed at Meren.

"Tell him to reveal the traps he set for my children," Meren ground out. "He's dying. The only thing that should concern him is his soul."

Zulaya's eyes opened wide, and he turned his face to Meren and laughed. "The ever honorable Meren." He wet his fingertips in his blood and touched Meren's lips. Meren jerked away, but not in time to avoid the blood. Zulaya laughed weakly again, and his hand dropped.

"I can't help it. For all your talent, riches, and beauty, the truth still escapes you. After all the blood," he said, "you still don't know who was behind it all."

"Don't try to avoid the judgment of the gods with your lies," Meren said. He pulled Zulaya up by his robe so that their faces were close together. "Tell me how to save my children, or by all the gods of creation, I'll pursue your soul to the depths of the underworld to see you suffer agonies beyond imagining."

Zulaya smiled as blood appeared between his lips, and he held Meren's gaze. "She betrayed us all when she reconciled with the priests of Amun. My doings were sanctioned by her evil."

Meren's shout filled the marketplace, but Zulaya paid him

no heed. The wounded man's gaze shifted to Anath, who held her breath as he gasped.

"My little jewel."

"Damn you, Zulaya!"

Meren watched with horror as life faded from the merchant's eyes. There was a rattling in his throat, and he died. Anath screamed and collapsed on her father's body, wailing.

Meren found it hard to stand, but he did. Desperation crowded out the pain of scrapes and aching muscles. It banished the humiliation and pain of Anath's betrayal. With an animal-like growl, he stooped and tore her from her father's body.

"It seems I'm too late to save you as you saved me."

Meren whirled around. Dragging Anath with him, he sank to the ground at the feet of the king. He hadn't even noticed the royal soldiers busy putting the market in order or understood the significance of the trumpet call. Tutankhamun stood beside his new chariot with his royal bodyguard arrayed behind him.

"Rise, Meren. I was driving my new chariot past Golden House, and Lady Bener accosted me with the news that the Eyes of Babylon had betrayed my majesty." Tutankhamun glared at Anath. "And you."

"My daughter, majesty?"

"Indeed. She feared the woman had lured you away for an evil purpose and that Kysen might be too late to prevent it." Tutankhamun walked over to look at Zulaya's body. "But you didn't need me at all."

"I am grateful for thy care, majesty."

"Who is this man?"

"He is called Zulaya, majesty, but once he was known as the Aten priest, Thanuro. It was he who committed the crime I was investigating for thy majesty, but there is an urgent matter I must resolve. I beg leave to question the Eyes of Babylon at once, Golden One, for Zulaya set traps for my children that were to spring if he was killed."

"Him?" The king fixed Zulaya's body with a stare so intense it should have burst into flames. *"At last,"* Tutankhamun breathed. Abruptly he turned to Meren without even glancing at Anath. "You may question her. I'll send reinforcements to Golden House for Bener's protection and send others to find Kysen. He went in search of you and by now he's probably on your trail."

Anath had stopped wailing. As the king spoke, she suddenly pulled the dagger from Zulaya's chest.

Meren shouted, "Majesty!"

Tutankhamun was already moving. His foot lashed out, hit Anath's arm, and knocked the knife free. She cried out in pain as Karoya leaped between the king and her and aimed his spear at her. The Nubian glanced at pharaoh, awaiting the order to kill.

"Give her to Meren," the king said. "When he's finished, my majesty would question the Eyes of Babylon before she dies."

Meren dragged Anath to a deserted beer stall and shoved her against it. Her tears had yet to dry, but she faced him without flinching. Meren had no interest in her daring.

Holding himself in check, Meren spoke with barely leashed violence. "Even I can't save you, but I may be able to persuade pharaoh to grant you a painless death. Help me protect my children, and I will intercede with him on your behalf."

Anath eyed him with hatred. "You killed my father as surely as if you wielded the knife yourself. I want to see you suffer as I do."

"Even at the price of your own agony." Meren grabbed her arms and lifted her so that her face was close to his. "In all your years abroad, have you forgotten what black horror awaits those whom pharaoh's wrath condemns?" He lowered his voice to a whisper. "If I have to, I'll cut off your fingers and toes one at a time and make you watch me feed them to his majesty's leopard."

At last he saw fear flicker in Anath's eyes.

"You know me," he said. "I give you my promise, and make this vow by the souls of my children. If you don't tell me what I want to know, I will make your death so horrible it will make the demons of the underworld piss with fright."

"Don't!" Anath began to struggle, and Meren released her. She fell against the beer stall and blurted out, "Nebra was in charge of the plans for your family. He was the one who was to decide whom to kill and when to do it. With him dead, you have nothing to fear."

"How do I know you're telling the truth?"

Anath straightened and gave him a sly look. "An excellent question. You'll never be certain unless I give you the names of Father's men. Persuade pharaoh to send me into exile instead of killing me, and I'll give you all of them."

Meren hesitated, but his answer was forestalled when Karoya came for them. They returned to the king.

"Majesty, Anath says she'll give us the names of all Zulaya's men if you will exile her instead of putting her to death."

"You know my answer to that, Meren."

"But, majesty—"

"No! She has betrayed my majesty and endangered the kingdom. She has plotted with one whose power threatened mine." Tutankhamun lashed his chariot whip against his thigh as he glared at Anath. "You will give me the names of Zulaya's men and reveal every plot and evil plan."

Meren dropped to his knees before the king. "Please, majesty. I fear for the lives of my children."

He bent down and touched his forehead to the ground before the king's feet. He heard the whip slap rhythmically, then the king ordered Anath taken away. Meren felt desperation begin to take hold of his thoughts. He was startled when Tutankhamun spoke again.

"Rise, Meren."

He stood and lifted his gaze to behold a chilly and ruthless youth. Abruptly the severity in the king's expression faded, and his voice softened.

"I will bargain with her for your sake."

"I am grateful beyond expression, majesty."

"You've nearly lost your life in my service once again. How could I not protect you and those close to you in return?" The king smiled at him. "Anath will suffer no harm while she is in my kingdom, and she will be sent into exile."

Meren bowed low to the king. As he did so Kysen and a complement of charioteers appeared across the marketplace. The king gave a string of orders and stalked to his chariot.

Kysen hurried over to Meren. "Father, you're all right? What happened? That's Zulaya." Understanding broke over him, and he looked at Zulaya's body again. "It was him?"

"Yes," Meren said. He was watching the king and Anath. She was on her knees before pharaoh, and when the king barked out an order, Karoya and another guard dropped to one knee and listened to their prisoner intently.

"What's happening?" Kysen asked.

"Not now, Ky. You shouldn't even be on your feet, much less out in the streets."

Karoya and the guard stood, saluted pharaoh, and vanished into the crowd. The king beckoned to Meren.

When Meren joined him, pharaoh nodded to Kysen and said, "My majesty is pleased to allow Mistress Anath to go into exile once it is proved she has revealed all the secrets of the traitor Zulaya. Until then she will be imprisoned."

Tutankhamun left them abruptly and motioned Kysen to accompany him. As Meren watched them go, he was suddenly aware of his misery and exhaustion. But he still had questions for Anath, though it cost him much to face her again. Released from fear for his children, however, he could no longer ignore the personal betrayal that lay between them. She had exposed him, and he hated feeling naked and defenseless. And it was painful to behold her fierceness, her courage, now that he knew she'd never loved him.

Holding himself in check, Meren spoke quietly. "Thanuro was your father?"

"Why are you surprised?" Anath snapped, bitterness etching lines around her mouth and eyes. "My mother was bound to an old man. Tell me you haven't served as a refuge and giver of pleasure to a young woman saddled with an ancient partner."

Meren had no answer to a commonplace problem. Young men were often without means to set up a household of their own. Older ones could afford to do so, and many refused to admit that affording the company of several women was not the same as making them happy.

"I can't believe that you committed treason and murder simply to help your father."

Anath snorted. "No, I don't suppose you can, you with your golden lineage and place at the right hand of the king. What did I have? Nothing but scraps from that old wreck of a man, until Fa—" A spasm of pain passed over her.

"But Ay trained you, gave you a position to which few women could aspire."

"He did that for his own ends, not for me. No one ever thought about me except Father. Did you?" Anath's voice trembled with animosity. "None of you cared how I felt about being a spy and a whore. Did you ever ask me what I wanted? I would have told you, back then, at Horizon of the Aten. Do you want to know now?" She spat at his feet. "I wanted to be like other girls, curse you. I wanted a husband and children and to be called mistress of the house, like any woman of honor and good birth. And because of Ay and the rest of you, I was denied all of that!"

Meren opened his mouth to refute her accusations, but no words came. How could he know what a young girl might feel in such a situation?

"You could have refused," he said.

Anath's eyes glittered, and she gave a sharp laugh. "Do you know what my choice was? I could accept Ay's offer, or marry an ancient nobleman my father insisted upon. He stank, Meren, and he had no teeth."

"I'm sorry," Meren said. "I didn't know."

"You didn't care. The only one who did was my real father. He tried to buy me from the old man, but he was refused. So I became one of the Eyes and Ears of Pharaoh." Anath bowed mockingly. "Your servant."

"And you've been Zulaya's ally all along."

"Why do you think I went to Babylon?"

Meren looked away. "So you came home to help him by spying on me."

"Did you know he admired you?" Anath's lips twisted in a parody of a smile. "When you began to investigate Nefertiti's death, he wasn't alarmed. He thought he would rid himself of you easily. Later, when you survived all that he threw at you, he began to respect you. I told him you were dangerous and that trying to control you was foolhardy, but he wouldn't listen. He wanted to keep you, like some kind of war trophy."

"And you wanted to kill me."

Anath met his eyes with resentment. "He was the only person besides my mother who ever really cared about me. *Me*, not the Eyes of Babylon. I didn't have to earn his good opinion or his affection. He loved me, and I was afraid for him. With good reason." She turned to gaze at her father's body, still lying on the packed earth of the market.

"I must know one thing." When she didn't respond, he continued. "Why did he poison the queen?"

"He never told me," Anath said. "I think she discovered he was spying on her for pharaoh and threatened to ruin him. None of you understood him. He was serving pharaoh by watching the queen and her daughters, protecting them against heresy and seeing that they didn't fall victim to misguided notions. It was long ago, and he must have had an overwhelming reason to kill her. She must have tried to harm him."

Vague dissatisfaction settled over Meren. At first he'd thought Zulaya was taunting him, trying to confuse him by saying he ought to know who was really behind the queen's murder. Now he wasn't so certain. Something was missing. Before he could follow this line of thought Anath suddenly moved into his arms and gave him an imploring look.

"Forgive me, Meren."

Meren took her wrists and gently disengaged himself. "You told me what was between us was false."

"Not all of it. I have always been fond of you, my love."

"I don't think so, Anath. One seldom contemplates killing one's true love."

"That was a mistake. I didn't know what I was doing."

Shaking his head, Meren said gently, "Anath, I think you've always known what you were doing. Right now you're worried I'll seek to avenge myself upon you, and you must have a low opinion of me if you think I'll succumb to you a second time."

"Ah, Meren." Anath faced him squarely, her gaze forthright. "You're wrong to think I have no feeling for you. I do admire you. How can I help it when we're so alike?" She sighed, her eyes filling with tears. "You're right. You're not a fool. But I would have won this battle of ours had it not been for a cat and a monkey. I think I wanted that victory more than anything I've ever wished for in my life. So you see, I do love you, in my way."

"I beg you to spare us both," Meren said in a choked whisper. Unable to bear watching her anymore, he signaled the royal guards. He kept his gaze fixed on a beer jar until he was certain she'd gone.

He was still staring at the jar when he heard an exclamation. Tutankhamun was kneeling on one knee beside Zulaya's body. Meren hurried to his side and dropped to the ground. Zulaya's robes were wet with blood, and through the hole left by the knife he could see part of a gold pendant suspended from a chain. A narrow shaft of gold ended in a stylized hand. Meren pulled the chain so that the necklace came free, knowing what he would find. Beneath his clothing Zulaya had worn the old symbol of the Aten— the sun disk with rays radiating from it that ended in those stylized hands. He exchanged startled looks with the king.

"After all these years," Tutankhamun said. "Why would he still carry the Aten disk?"

"Perhaps he was a true follower of thy majesty's brother, Golden One."

Tutankhamun pulled the necklace over Zulaya's head, rose, and stood examining it. The sun disk had been set in a hollow gold frame, and several of the stylized hands and rays were smeared with blood. The boy's eyes took on that distant look of one who is lost in memory, and his hand closed over the sun disk, squeezing it hard.

"It is unfortunate that he was killed so quickly," the king said. "An easy death hardly serves my majesty's justice."

"He will face the vengeance of the gods in the Hall of Judgment, majesty."

"No!" Tutankhamun hurled the necklace to the ground. "I am pharaoh. It is for me to condemn and destroy traitors. I wanted him to face my vengeance!"

Meren bowed low as the king swore, got into his chariot, and drove out of the market, his face set. He thought about following and trying to ease the boy's temper, but the shine of the gold necklace caught his eye. He picked it up. Slowly, with hesitation, he removed the wristband that covered the scar on his arm. He gazed at the white flesh distorted into the same hated symbol as the one Zulaya had worn.

I am pharaoh. It is for me to condemn and destroy traitors. Had Akhenaten been pharaoh, Meren would have been the traitor, not Zulaya.

"Pharaoh," Meren muttered to himself. Then the necklace dropped through fingers gone suddenly cold. "Pharaoh!"

Around him soldiers helped vendors right overturned stalls. Others guided Anath's chariot away, but Meren saw nothing. Zulaya had been telling the truth. Meren had known who was behind the murder of the queen all along.

Many had a reason to fear the great royal wife, but there had been one whose fury would have been unparalleled. The one whom she betrayed. The one who had already killed the old gods of Egypt, and thus would not hesitate to order the death of a mere queen.

"Akhenaten," Meren whispered.

Zulaya had said it himself as he died—Nefertiti betrayed pharaoh by reconciling with Amun. Zulaya had found out and told the king, and Akhenaten had ordered him to kill his wife. Meren knew only too well how Akhenaten dealt with members of his court who failed to adhere solely to the Aten.

The murder had been designed so that the manner of her death concealed how his own wife had betrayed pharaoh. And Akhenaten had played the devastated royal husband with sickening accuracy.

No wonder Thanuro had left the royal court and arranged his own death. He had feared Akhenaten, and with good reason. No king would tolerate the existence of one who knew such a secret. Undoubtedly Akhenaten had been quite willing to see Thanuro go.

Feeling ill, Meren heard his name called. Kysen was coming toward him accompanied by several royal bodyguards. He lifted a hand in salute. Everything around him seemed unreal. It was the shock of the truth that made him feel as if the ground was crumbling beneath his feet. What was he going to tell Ay? He'd meant to tell his old mentor everything once he'd exposed the murderer. Could he tell the fragile old man that the husband he'd chosen for his daughter had ordered her death?

"Wait," Meren said as Kysen walked up to him. He held his hand up for silence and walked away. He went back to the beer stall, picked up a jar with a strainer, and poured beer into a cup the beer seller held out to him. He drained the cup and wiped his lips.

For years he'd suspected that Ay had had knowledge of

Akhenaten's sudden and unexplained death. Had Ay discovered his daughter had been murdered and avenged her? Meren griped the edge of the stall while he followed this line of reasoning. Ay might have known all along that Akhenaten was to blame. This explained why he'd sent Meren away, so that he could devise the death of a pharaoh.

And Meren dared not ask him for the truth. All he had was suspicion. He had no real proof that Akhenaten had been the one who commanded Thanuro to kill the queen. Meren closed his eyes, and his shoulders drooped.

His inquiry must come to a halt. To pursue it further risked chaos, and Egypt had suffered enough. Tutankhamun had endured too much. Meren wasn't going to be the one to tell him that the murderer of Nefertiti was Akhenaten, Slayer of Gods.

Drawing himself up, Meren straightened and walked back to the waiting men. Kysen searched his face, and Meren smiled bleakly. As he gazed at his son, the weight on his soul lifted. The long ordeal was over, and justice of a sort had been accomplished. He might have played the fool along the way, but personal humiliation was nothing compared to restoring rightness and order. Anath's betrayal was a raw wound, and he needed a healing salve.

"Kysen, I'm going to visit Tefnut. We're all going. With any luck, I'll reach her in time for the birth of her first child."

"A great event," Kysen said.

Meren grasped Wind Chaser's bridle and stroked his nose. "Indeed, my son. And one that will renew my ka, which has been sorely tried of late." They got into the chariot, and Meren slapped the reins. "Oh, and Ky, remind me to send someone to drag old Dilalu out of hiding. If I forget, he'll stay underground like a fat old scorpion and then escape completely."

Turning the chariot around, Meren drove out of the market leaving the body of Zulaya to the royal guards, and the flies.